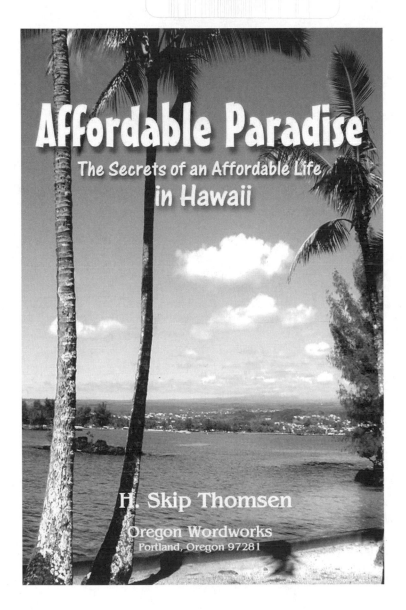

Affordable Paradise

The Secrets of an Affordable Life

in Hawaii

H. Skip Thomsen

Oregon Wordworks
Portland, Oregon 97281

Affordable Paradise
The Secrets to an Affordable Life in Hawaii

Copyright © 2003 Oregon Wordworks
ISBN: 0-9719185-0-3
Third Edition, 2005

By H. Skip Thomsen
Edited by Camille Thomsen

Cover art, layout, and design by the author.
All photographs by the author, except as noted.

Published by:
OREGON WORDWORKS
P.O. Box 231091, Portland, OR 97281
www.mailbooks.com

Printed in the USA

Limits of Liability and Disclaimer
This book is based on years of experiences and observations of the author and the many people interviewed during the writing process. The author shall not be held liable in any event for incidental or consequential damages in connection with or arising out of the use of information contained in this book.

Table of Contents

Acknowledgements

I wish to express my gratitude to the entirety of the Island of Hawai'i: her many people who have both knowingly and unknowingly contributed to the creation of this book; her awesome *Mana, 'Aina and Aloha,* without which there would have been no need for this book; and to my bride (and Editor!), Camille, who gave her unfailing support in every phase of the project.

Mahalo Nui!

Skip Thomsen

Introduction

The focus of the first and second editions of *Affordable Paradise* was primarily dispelling the myths of how expensive it is to live in Hawai'i. In the four short years since the publication of that first edition, real estate prices in Hawai'i have risen dramatically. This factor alone has certainly put a dent in the "affordable" part of living in Hawai'i, but the myths about every other aspect of the cost of living here are still alive and well. We'll address those.

First off, I would like to make two things clear. One is that this book is in no way a blanket invitation to move to Hawai'i. Rather, it is speaking to those folks who have already pretty much decided to make the move, and now need some credible information that seems to be missing from the other "Hawai'i books."

The second point is that this book is about the Big Island; the Island called Hawai'i. There still seems to be some confusion about which Island is the Big Island, and it is surprising to us how many people just assume that the "Big Island" must be where Honolulu and Waikiki Beach are located. Not!

Those two places, famous to every tourist and would-be tourist, are on the Island of Oahu. The Island of Oahu is tiny compared to the Big Island. Matter of fact, all of the other major Hawai'ian Islands would fit nicely on the Big Island with room to spare. Curiously, the population of Honolulu, just one city in corner of the Island of Oahu, has over twice as many residents as the entire Big Island. That might give you a sense of the difference in population densities.

The first two editions of this book have received some criticism regarding this focus is on the Big Island. "How is this book going to help me if I want to move to Maui?" they ask. Well, it isn't. It isn't any more than if I had written a book about the most affordable places to live on the Mainland and you ask me "How is this book going to help me if I want to live in San Francisco?" The book is on how to live affordably in Hawai'i, so to that end, it does not cover the places in Hawai'i that transcend affordability in every dimension.

For a number of reasons, there are hordes of people moving to Hawai'i right now, and especially to the Big Island. The increase in population in our beloved little city of Hilo is very noticeable, especially to those of us who live here full time. Where three years ago, four cars at a stoplight was about as close as we got to a traffic jam, we now have real commuter traffic, sometimes bumper-to-bumper. The Kona-side traffic has become impossible. Well, maybe not to mainland folks who are used to five-mile commutes that take 45 minutes, but to those of us who have lived here for years, it is worrisome.

Parking lots are now jammed to capacity at all hours of the day. The up-side of this population boom is, that in many areas, our wonderful assortment of small businesses ranging from espresso shops to furniture stores and everything in between, are just now starting to see some profits. Although all the new people are certainly helping this situation with their patronage, in Hilo and Kailua, every parking place is taken all day, every day. There are constantly cars slowly cruising around, just hoping that somebody will turn loose of a parking spot. This is all so very different from only two years ago.

East Hawai'i's beautiful agricultural lands are being subdivided into enormously expensive (by Hawai'i standards) residential lots. These lots sell as soon as they appear on the market, and each time another subdivision is complete, the prices have gone up again. Twenty-acre lots that two years ago seemed overpriced at $200,000 are now bringing twice that amount—and more.

If this all sounds like the days of affordable housing are over, do not despair! There are still many beautiful areas that have been overlooked by the masses. We'll show you where to find them.

So why would anyone want to move here any more? Well, that's what this book is all about, only this edition will focus way more on the philosophical areas of moving to and living in Hawai'i than on the nuts-and-bolts of actually getting here. Sure, we still cover these things, but there are already lots of other books on the shelves that will give you that information, so we'll keep our version to what we feel the others have overlooked. You can find additional recommended reading at the back of this book.

When we speak of the philosophical areas of moving to and living in Hawai'i, we speak mainly of **aloha**. We speak of the ever-increasing need for all of us to live lives of aloha. What it comes down to is that those of us who understand and appreciate what Hawai'i is truly about must graciously accept our responsibility to educate the newcomers to what it really means to live and love in Hawai'i. We will also speak to the importance of supporting and honoring Hawai'ians and the Hawai'ian culture, and in doing so, deepening our understanding and appreciation of aloha. We are, after all, their guests in these magical Islands.

Aloha Nui!

SKIP THOMSEN & OHANA

Chapter One

The Dream

Aloha is alive and well!

There's a magical, special feeling in these Islands of Hawai'i. Those of us who live here call it aloha. It's alive and well, and to some it's so powerful and pervasive that it soon becomes an essential part of life. To many people, this feeling is a huge part of what they're here for. Perhaps they're even here for healing or for a specific spiritual focus, but in any event it's the mystique and power of the Islands that brings them to this extraordinary destination in the first place, and in the end it is what keeps them here forever.

To others, these feelings seem not to exist. We've had friends from the mainland come to visit and notice nothing, while others feel it profoundly. We even had one friend say that she surely feels the ambiance of love and acceptance here but she thought it was some kind of tourist-trickery being played by the Visitor's Bureau! And she was serious!

The more obvious draw of this Island is its natural resources: the pristine beaches, the crystal clear ocean, the awesome and varied flora, and of course the spectacular volcano. A less obvious but no less important draw is the mana, or spiritual power. The Big Island is home and host to many spiritual events, sessions, celebrations, and workshops from many differing disciplines. The Zen Temple in Wood Valley hosts these kinds of events all year long, and others take place in less formal surroundings, like in some of the sacred and powerful places all over this Island or perhaps even on a quiet beach. The Magic is one of the big reasons why so many people are drawn here for their spiritual work. It's somehow so easy in The Islands.

Each of us sees "the Dream" differently. To some, it's being able to spend lots of time on beautiful white sand beaches and never again having to think about "going back home." To others, it's the sumptuous weather and never again having to burn anything to keep warm. Or it's the quiet, gracious, simple and unhurried lifestyle. And to others still, it's as simple as this: It feels good. It feels good to every one of our senses, psychological, physical and spiritual.

To us, it is all of these things. It is somehow so easy and natural to stay grounded here, and there is just "something in the air" that is a constant, gentle reminder that keeps us on our spiritual path. This is a simple life where friends matter more than timetables, where inner peace and aloha come easy.

It feels so good to us to be among these wonderful people of many cultures who all seem to be of one big, loving family. The color of your skin, the kind of car you drive, the size of your home—none of these things matter here. What's in your heart is all that matters.

This is a generalization, but we believe those who end up staying here are the people who Know in their Knowingness the minute they first breathe the sweet, sensuous air of the Islands that they have come home and that this is where they must be.

The Change to Island-Style

It's interesting to observe our new friends and neighbors as they fall into step with Island life. It's especially interesting to watch the women who came from a professional life in some big city. At first, they find it awkward to shed the all-important apparel they've become so used to and adapt to the comfortable attire of the Islands. It's not too long, though, before they find real pleasure in their new comfort of pareos and rubber slippers. Even the makeup that was an everyday routine starts to become less important.

Men, too, take a while to adapt. But pretty soon the rubber slippers and shorts feel natural and they can laugh at the clothes they used to wear to keep up with the styles in the city. And then they wonder why it took so long.

Another interesting observation is how most people simply slow down. Those who talk fast, move fast and come from life in the fast lane are the most dramatic to watch. From the frenetic pace they brought with them, they begin the beautiful and healthy process of slowing down every nuance of their lives. Speech slows down and becomes more focused, mannerisms become more graceful and at ease, attention to others becomes more deliberate and loving, and they begin, consciously or not, to live aloha.

The People

In the Islands, and particularly in the rural areas, people always have time for friends, neighbors and even strangers. There's a popular pastime here called "talk story." You always have time to talk story. If you're ready to leave your home to go on an errand and a friend shows up, you stop what you're doing and talk story. You share a cup of coffee, tea or whatever, but you always have time. That's why sometimes appointments seem to have little meaning here. The bottom line is that people are more important than anything else.

Speaking of people, one of the things we love about living here is that everybody is a minority. There is no prejudice here; what your personal culture is doesn't matter. Again, it's what's inside that counts. This is especially true here on the Windward side of The Big Island, where the population is a wonderful mix of Hawai'ian, Chinese, Japanese, Filipino, Portuguese, haole (Caucasian), various Island cultures and others, and the beautiful results of the mixes of all of them. There is an obvious respect for everyone's culture, and each practices it's own ways to whatever extent they wish. And for those who have heard stories of how "the locals all dislike haoles" and other exceptions to this notion, we'll discuss that in detail in Chapter 2.

The Hawai'ian culture is alive and well here and is being preserved and nurtured. It's truly heartwarming to us every time we see another example of the energy that the young people here, especially the Hawai'ian kids of all ages, put into the preservation of their culture. The Hawai'ian culture is built upon love and acceptance, family and friends, the land and the ocean, and to a large extent, the Hula and music. These are the important things; everything else is secondary. There are lots of Hawai'ian cultural events here, and we recommend attending as many as possible. It's good to continue to learn about the culture and the ways of the people who are our hosts here in these Islands, and to maintain the highest possible respect for this amazing place and its people.

The cultural events we speak of are those put on by the local folks. There are theater events, street parties, talks by Hawai'ian elders, museums, musical events of all descriptions and even small Luaus and other informal gatherings where you can learn about local ways by observation and becoming involved. With a few exceptions, the so-called cultural productions by hotels and other tourist endeavors are not among our recommendations for really learning about Hawai'ian ways or history.

A large part of the Hawai'ian culture is based in the philosophy of giving back to the community. Those who live this philosophy would feel incomplete living their lives only for themselves, or even just for their own families. Family members give back to their families, and the family as a whole gives back to the community, and this, coming from the heart, is an important ingredient of the spirit of aloha. This is a philosophy not often found to be practiced in Mainland haole cultures and it is one of the differences not easily understood by the Hawai'ians. Not surprisingly, the Island haoles who truly live lives of aloha are those who find themselves most at ease with— and accepted by—the locals.

The dream of living in these Islands has as many interpretations as there are dreamers, and no one interpretation is less real than any other to the one doing the dreaming. There are few places on Earth that cast this kind of spell on their guests. If you are one of the dreamers, take heart! If it is truly your desire, you can live that dream.

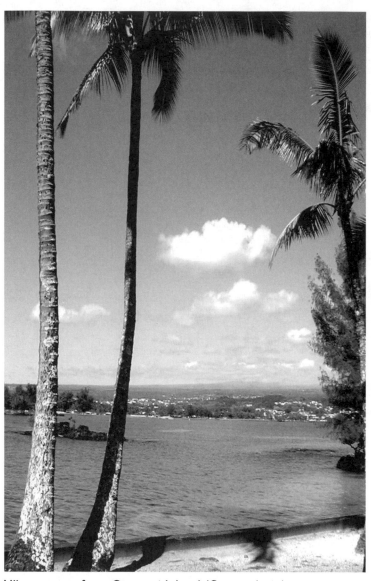

Hilo as seen from Coconut Island (Cover photo)

Chapter Two

The Realities

This chapter is where *Affordable Paradise* takes on a new spin from the previous editions. Even in the first edition, it had been suggested that we omit the whole chapter because it was "too negative."

From the beginning, we have always felt that this is essential information to anyone contemplating a move to Hawai'i, but in light of the incredible number of people who are now moving here from all over the mainland, the significance has grown exponentially.

As you read this chapter, please try your best to "feel" what you are reading. If necessary, read it more than once. "Feel" the situations we describe. Place yourself into the picture and see if it makes you uncomfortable. Try to feel what it would be like to experience the situations on a day-to-day basis.

It is so very important to realize that moving to Hawai'i is much like moving to a foreign country. Many people who come here with stars in their eyes soon begin to complain about how things are done here and how they differ from how they're done on the mainland.

Would you go to England and complain to the locals there about how stupid it is to drive on the left side of the road? How about moving to France and complaining about how hard it is to understand the English spoken by the French?

Our goal is to create in our readers a sense of Island life. Not "Island life" as you might perceive it while on a two-week vacation at some Hawai'i resort, but Island life as it is for your hosts here: the people who live here, love here, work here and raise their families here. The people who would live nowhere else on this planet; the people who although they have been here forever, never let a day go by without giving thanks for the privilege of being able to live in Paradise.

It is also to leave no doubt as to the importance of living aloha; living in a way that includes giving back to the community, to your neighbors, and to the people of these Islands who are your hosts. As more and more people flood in from every corner of the US mainland, we are beginning to see a dilution of aloha and it hurts. We are beginning to see the influence of a greater number of people who are bringing their mainland ways with them instead of leaving them behind.

We cannot stress it enough: If you are attracted to Hawai'i because of the beautiful aloha energy of her people, you must learn to live aloha. Of course, there are certainly lots of people who have been living aloha all their lives, no matter where they have been living. Those are the ones who will find it the easiest to blend into the Island culture and be accepted immediately.

Please feel the essence of what we are sharing with you, and we ask from our hearts that you take it seriously.

A lot of people love to travel and to experience the vastly differing lifestyles of other cultures. People come to Hawai'i and are impressed and intrigued by the lifestyle of this Island culture. They are blown away by the easy-going attitudes, the wonderful weather, and of course the pervasive spirit of aloha. They love it! They love it so much, in fact, that they decide to leave the mainland behind and move to the Islands.

Every day, folks come here and are enchanted by the magical feelings of these Islands, and some decide they just have to live here. Some of them decide too soon. They pack their belongings into a shipping container and move on over, and in a few months or maybe a year, they discover that this isn't "America." It's really much more like living in a foreign country, with a very different culture, and that culture comes with a different attitude and a different energy than that of most places on the Mainland. A lot of the locals here refer to the Mainland as "America," and prefer to think of the Hawai'ian Islands as a separate country. Their separate country. Not wishing to get into a lengthy political discussion here, there are certainly lots of good and valid reasons for their preference.

We use the term "locals" to refer to the people who have lived in the Islands for most or all of their lives. Locals can be of any culture or race, too, and that even includes haole.

In many ways, some subtle and others not-so-subtle, things work differently here. If the way they work fits in with your temperament, there's a good chance you'll find Hawai'i to be your special place. It's a very laid-back lifestyle, and if you can live with that and love it, it's a good start. But there's much more to it than that.

Indeed, it is the "laid back" part that attracts a lot of folks at first, but then in the end it can be some of the ingredients of "laid back" that seem to be their undoing.

This is a Test . . .

In this chapter we're going to share a few of the reasons some people turn tail and head back for the Mainland after trying Island life for a while. Some friends who read the manuscript suggested we leave out this chapter; that it is too negative. Well, that's why it's called "The Realities." Actually, it's rare when two or more people who observe the same situation come away with the same "reality," and your own reality of life in Hawai'i will be yours alone. Much depends on your own values and perceptions, so what we are sharing in this chapter (and indeed, in this book) are some of the things you need to "feel" for yourself. If the situations and word pictures we conjure up feel good to you, that's great. If they don't, we recommend a thoughtful evaluation on why not. If they don't feel good now, will they become major irritations later? Life in rural Hawai'i is not the same as a vacation at Waikiki Beach, and we would like you to be able to make a decision that will keep your heart smiling for a very long time.

A Little Story

Is the Dream real? How do we know if the dream is real or if we are just temporarily infatuated with the lure of the Islands?

Some time ago, we met a woman who had recently bought this beautiful home on a nicely manicured acre of tropical forest. She was fresh over from the Mainland and apparently quite taken with the property when she looked it over several times before the purchase, and appeared to be really excited about her decision to move to Hawai'i. She went back home, had all her belongings packed and shipped over and arrived in her new home. The sellers had left it immaculately clean, with gorgeous flowers everywhere. There were even orchids floating in the toilets, a kind of aloha tradition. The sellers had also made her a gift of quite a bit of furniture to ease her transition and make her comfortable until her container arrived.

Much to our surprise, it wasn't a month later when we heard her start complaining about a few things. Some things about the house, the location, the rain in particular and the weather in general. When she started in on the people, we knew she wouldn't be here long. Everywhere she went, she came upon "that local attitude," mostly because people didn't do things the way she had come to expect from her Mainland experiences. Eventually, she became bitter about nearly everything, and finally sold her house and moved back to America. We hear similar versions of this story all the time.

Here's another little story, but with a different twist. A couple we got to know pretty well had moved over from California. They were both totally enchanted with what they felt of Hawai'i on their trips over, and as with so many others, they simply packed up and moved over.

Here in the Islands, most people enjoy finding it difficult to avoid making new friends at a rapid rate. On the flip side, we've heard from some folks who sense the open friendliness here as an invasion of their privacy.

So this couple was here for several months and we could feel that something was not right with them. They told us of a mild feeling of depression in one of them, mostly because of a feeling of isolation and not knowing anyone here. We, as did the few other mutual friends of ours and theirs, did our best to introduce them to others here so that they could expand their "friend-pool."

It didn't work. One of them made friends easily, but the other did not. She continued to place her attention on her loneliness instead of on all the friendly people around her. She felt so isolated here, and eventually the overriding energy all around her forced her decision to head back to the comfort zone of their old environs.

Yet another story. Isn't this fun? We recently rented a furnished house to a woman and her husband from the mainland. When we prepare a furnished house, it is way beyond what any reasonable person might expect to find. Every detail in this beautiful home was attended to. The whole place had been newly repainted inside, most of the furnishings were brand new and of high quality, all of the appliances were new, the kitchen had just been fully remodeled, there was lots of tasteful art on the walls, there was a big TV in a beautiful, handcrafted entertainment center, and when the guests arrived, there was sweet Hawai'ian music playing on the stereo, the ceiling fans were gently turning, and there were beautiful tropical flowers in the living room. The place was bright, sunny and just delightful.

This guest, in one of several phone calls before she arrived, asked how many beds there were. I told her there was a king in the master bedroom, two twins in the second bedroom and one twin made up into a day-bed in the third bedroom. She was renting the place for two people, yet she told me, "I'm going to need a futon bed in that third bedroom so my guests' kids will have a place to sleep." Then she told my wife, Camille she would also need a second TV in the bedroom, as she liked to watch TV in bed.

Not being the typical landlord, Camille immediately bought and installed a new $500 futon bed as requested, and a second, also new, TV in the bedroom.

It was finally the day when this couple arrived, and I got the honor of escorting them from the airport to the house. The first communication with this woman was when I met her at the airport, when she firmly chastised me for keeping her waiting for a few minutes. That was my first red flag. Then when we arrived at this sweet home (with a gorgeous ocean view, by the way), she walked into the house with a disgruntled look on her face, complained about there not being a dishwasher, complained about there not being a hand-held shower in the bathroom, and then her husband started in on how hard it was going to be for him to find work in this place where "there are no jobs." Not one positive word came from either of them. Not one tiny acknowledgement about the condition of this home or how beautifully and lovingly it was prepared for them.

The next day, she called to complain that I had not yet installed her hand-held shower, and told me that they had gone to Richardson Beach and what kind of people would call that place a "beach?" And the water was murky and cold.

Gosh, Richardson Beach Park is our favorite place to go swimming and snorkeling! It has a long-standing reputation as one of the best snorkeling spots on the Island because of the incredibly clear water. (We really do each create or own reality.)

My point in all this is simple: These folks most likely will not make it here. Their energy is so far afield from the energy that makes Hawai'i what it is, that in a short time, they'll simply leave. Their discontent will continue to grow until they won't be able to tolerate it any more. And they'll have lots of interesting stories to tell their friends back on the Mainland about what an inhospitable place Hawai'i is.

Here's a reprint of the article on "Attitudes" that we recently published to the *Affordable Paradise* Web site. If we're coming off as a bit over-the-top on this topic, please be assured that it is of the utmost importance for folks contemplating a life in Hawai'i to fully feel this situation in their hearts and minds.

This Special Report is inspired by the huge numbers of people who are "discovering" East Hawai'i and rushing to buy homes here . . . often for the wrong reasons.

Hawai'i is about people. As a comparison, one might say that California's infamous Silicon Valley is about money and the things money can buy. Of course, both of these concepts are generalizations, but they begin the painting of an essential picture of Hawai'i.

Hawai'i is about love, friendship, peace of mind, and most important of all, aloha. Aloha includes love, friendship and peace of mind, but is also far more than that. Aloha is a feeling so powerful; to some people it is nearly overwhelming, yet to others it seems to be just another word-maybe coined by the Hawai'i Visitor's Bureau.

Do you feel a special feeling around Christmastime where you live now? Not too many years ago, even in the hearts of the big cities, there was just "something in the air." It remains today, but probably not as pervasive as it once was. People just seem to be more friendly, more open. They take the time to greet others on the street, make eye contact where at other times they were too preoccupied with other things to bother.

That feeling is a very brief description of what aloha feels like all year long. In the Hawai'ian tradition, it is essential to give back to your community. It is a part of everyone's life to give of themselves, not only to their families and friends, but to the community and to the land and the sea. There is no word in the Hawai'ian language for "consumer."

How does all this relate to the topic of attitudes? Aloha is the foundation of the attitude of the Islands. Mainland attitudes are, with some exceptions of course, quite different. Some of the exceptions are that generally, the more rural the area you hail from, the more closely your community's attitude might resemble Island attitude. Conversely, the more densely populated your community is, the less likely it is that you get to enjoy anything similar to Island attitude.

Let me tell you a little story. We have been managing 14 vacation rentals for a while now, and believe it or not, conservatively 90% of our rental guests are here looking for property. Many of those looking actually buy something before they return home. This means we're getting a lot of new people here, and the increased auto traffic all over the Island is testimony to that fact. Fortunately, the great majority of the newcomers are terrific people who feel Hawai'i in their hearts and just know in their knowingness that they must be here. But there have been a few who are not of that kind.

We have seen a few folks come here from the fast-money places on the Mainland and when they see the reasonable prices of homes here, all they can think of is profit. Making a fast buck off of the next guy who comes along. To them, Hawai'i is just another place, but one in which they feel they can make some easy money.

I like to use this anecdote: Hawai'i has been said to be a cruel hostess to those who should not be here. We have seen examples of this over and over. We used to just listen to stories from Hawai'ian friends about how Madam Pele, the Volcano Goddess, has taken care of the profiteers. We've seen the results of that, too. But we have seen even more in-our-faces results of people who have come here for the fast buck. They don't stay long, because for some reason they cannot understand, they simply can't make things work for themselves here as they are used to on the Mainland.

We've seen people come here and get into a frenzy to buy themselves a vacation rental. When asked if they were planning on retiring here one day, they would say, oh no, we just see how we can buy this place for nearly nothing down and have the rental guests pay for it, and that is good real estate wealth-building practice.

There are few logical explanations for the ultimate failure of most of these kinds of ventures, but after living here for years, we can almost always see it coming. Often the first signs are when these profit-oriented people start complaining about how things work here. The next phase will be the complaints about how difficult it is to get anything done right. How undependable and incompetent they think the local workers are.

We're experienced vacation rentals that simply won't book. The photos look fine in their Internet presentations-maybe even better than others on the same Web site, but nobody ever inquires about them.

Why is that? Again, no logical explanation. Things just work differently here. We believe that most people can feel things from their hearts that they never become really conscious of, among them perhaps some negative energy from an Internet presentation. They don't stop to ask, "Why do I feel this way?" Somehow, it just doesn't feel good and they go on to something else.

We've tried our best to explain this phenomenon to people we saw were clearly heading down this un-aloha path, and they probably thought we were nuts. Psycho-babble, right? We've also seen lava flows take out areas exactly as predicted by the local Hawai'ian elders after their warnings of improper development went unheeded.

No logical explanation.

Hawai'i is a very special place. It is a place of awesome mana (spiritual power), and we encourage those who feel and honor the mana to respectfully investigate the possibilities for themselves here. But with all due respect for those who do not, we encourage them to seek other environs. We encourage all to honor the Hawai'ian tradition of giving back to the community, which means way more than simply not seeing Hawai'i as a potential for financial profit. That is certainly one aspect of it, however.

One big reason for this book is a reality-check to those folks who were coming here anyway. I get quite a bit of terrific feedback from readers, and the folks for whom I feel I have done the greatest service are those who tell me that after reading the book, they changed their minds about moving here. A failed effort to "live in Paradise" can be an emotionally devastating experience, especially to those who search for reasons.

Moving right along . . .

Doing business in Hawai'i

Do you wear glasses? Well, here's a little story that is typical of many encounters with the business community here. Now, as hard as this is going to be, I don't want you to take this story as "complaining." It isn't. It's just a little vignette of how things happen a lot here, and the purpose of the story is to get you, the reader, to FEEL the situation. Feel yourself in the story and then feel your reaction. Anxiety? Anger? A good laugh?

Three months ago I decided that my old lenses were now scratched up enough that they needed to be replaced. My frames had seen too much salt (we spend a lot of time at—and in—the ocean.) and the hinges were corroded, so a whole new pair of specs was in order.

I went to a local purveyor of eyeglasses, got my prescription checked, perused the limited frame selection, and settled for a simple but expensive frame and proceeded to order up the lenses. I paid the bill in full, the man said, "Fine, you should have your new glasses in two weeks. I'll call you when they come in."

Three weeks later, I was in the neighborhood so I stopped in to see if my new glasses had arrived. "Sure did," said the man at the desk, and he disappeared through a back door only to come back with somebody else's glasses.

"What's your name?" he then asked. I told him and he looked me up on his computer. As his brow furrowed, he told me that I didn't seem to be on his computer at all and that he simply couldn't understand that. Now remember, this was the very same guy who I had been working with all along. Then he started looking through all the drawers in his desk and guess what?! There was an envelope with my name on it! Yes! My glasses!

I didn't want to confuse the issue by asking how that had happened, so I said nothing. He simply handed my the envelope and said, "There you are. Thank you."

"What," I thought to myself, "no fitting? No adjustment?" So I took the new glasses out of the envelope and tried them on. The frames didn't even come close to fitting my face, and looking through the right lens was like looking through a fog. I asked him if he would be so kind as to fit the frames to me and he took them, twisted them into a pretzel, and handed them back to me. He had actually improved the fit, and I figured I could finish the job on my own.

I told him about the fog, and he told me that I needed some time to adjust to the new prescription and to give it a week or so. After more decades than I wish to count of wearing glasses, you can bet I've heard that one a few times!

One week later: The fog persisted. My old glasses, scratches and all, were far better than the "new improved" version. I took them back and the nice man said, "No problem. I'll send them back and you should have the new ones in another two to three weeks." I asked how come it took longer to fix them than it took to make them in the first place. He didn't know, that's just the way it was. Well, alright.

Three weeks later, I went in and asked about my glasses. This time the fellow who had always been there was not, and a young woman told me he was on a short vacation and she was filling in for him. So I asked, well, can you check to see if my glasses have come in? She looked through all the desk drawers, couldn't find anything with my name on it so she tried calling the manager on his cell phone. Turns out his cell was out of range, so the nice young woman told me my glasses would no doubt be in by the following Wednesday. The following Friday I went back in and the same young woman was there. This time she found my glasses, and in only the second desk drawer!

Well, folks, I finally had my new glasses, complete with that pesky fog. I've been trying to wear them now for a week and they're going to have to go back. Either the prescription was incorrect or the lenses were not ground to the prescription. (Or maybe they were the same glasses they gave me the first time?) Either way, I'll have to start from scratch.

My point? This scenario is one of those that would make many folks from the Mainland go ballistic. People on the Mainland are definitely not used to this kind of performance from a business, let alone a "professional." And although there certainly are professionals here who are indeed professional and competent, there certainly are some exceptions.

Need a building permit? Our County Building Department has a well-deserved reputation for being difficult to work with. It seems that some of the folks in charge feel that it is their calling to make things as difficult as possible. If you have worked with Mainland building departments where the folks in charge regularly do their professional best to see that your experience with them is as painless and efficient as possible, the "Island Way" might test your patience to the limit.

For many years, we've been hearing stories of how "things just don't happen here the way they did back home." Surprise! This isn't back home. This is an Island in the middle of the ocean. This is the most remote land mass on the entire planet. Why should it "be like home?"

One of the big attractions of Hawai'i is exactly that it is NOT like "back home." So then why are these people surprised—and disappointed—to have the notion confirmed for them that Hawai'i is indeed different.

We've wondered why one of the differences seems to manifest itself as incompetence and indifference, especially in the business environment. In most cases, what comes across as incompetence is more often an unfamiliar process. Or the same process, but handled differently. For one thing, in the Island culture, the sense of urgency that accompanies many—if not most— Mainland business transactions is simply not felt. Perhaps one reason is that way out here in the middle of the ocean, it is often hard to find the supplies, tools or expertise needed to do a job in what Mainlanders would consider a timely manner. So if you're in the middle of remodeling your kitchen and when you go to buy your new appliances and you're told the ones you want will have to come from off-Island, what are you going to do? Have a fit, or go do something else for a while?

What we strive for here is a lifestyle that precludes needing anything in a hurry. Delays are just more opportunities to head for the beach. And so what if it takes an extra two or three weeks to finish painting the house? What's the hurry?

A few weeks ago, I needed an answer to a simple building-code question. I called the County Building Department, and after getting two more numbers to call (I seemed to always have reached "the wrong department"), I ended up with another voice-mail. I left a message and was certainly not surprised when after a week I got no reply. But here's the curious part: I called again, same number I called the first time, and got a polite secretary who handed off the call to a gentleman who immediately answered my question. Why the difference between the first and second and second attempts? Who knows . . .

An hour ago, I needed some info from our local Sears store. I called the "main information" number in the phone book. The phone rang and rang . . . no answer. No voice-mail, no answering machine. ***And this is Sears!*** Sears, Island Style. Ya gotta laugh!

That's the way it is here. Things don't happen here the way they do in most other places, nor are they supposed to.

We genuinely love it.

The remarkable thing is that some of the most unlikely businesses here are operated efficiently and effectively, with terrific attention to customer relations. The little operation that hauls away our weekly trash is an example. It actually seems that the smaller the business, the more likely you are to receive great, dependable service. But then, that is distinctly not always the case, either!

Enter the Extreme!

OK, this *is* pretty extreme, but I'd like to share with you some comments that were published in a magazine. They were rebuttals to an article on Hawai'i that I had written in the same magazine some time ago. I want you to experience the feelings some folks have about life in Hawai'i. These are actual excerpts from the published rebuttals (typos, misspellings, and all).

". . .the continual flights of helicopters overhead, searching for marijuana in everyone's backyard, are to say the least a major annoyance. The drug cops are so bold as to fly low and peer into the windows of your home. My wife has some nice photos of them trying to get a look at her while dressing one morning!

If they spot any growth, they either spray an agent orange type substance to kill the plants, or repel down and harvest the crop. Keep in mind, most home water supply in this area is by means of open air catchment systems. There are numerous reports from residents of ill side effects, on themselves, their livestock and anything they may be trying to grow."

Each of us creates his or her own reality, and that writer certainly had a reality vastly different from ours. We have heard of a few isolated stories of helicopter marijuana searches, but this one is a bit of a stretch.

Here's another person's reality:

"I spent about 2½ years in Hawai'i while on military assignment (now thankfully over) a paradise, a wonderful, tropical, beautiful place, you would think—I suppose—but, in truth, there is a much darker side to the sun & fun. (Although I was only on the Big Island about a dozen times— It was for 20-35 days at a stretch.)...

For instance, while I was there, I went thru 2 hurricanes, 2 volcano eruptions that we had to evacuate civilians, and caused a chopper to go down, witnessed a shark attack by a Tiger shark 13½ ft long. And read about many more in the paper—(I think 5 in one season—not year) saw a murder, read about many more, been thru a couple volcanic earthquakes, my now ex-wife, transvestites by the truck load—and semi-legalized prostitution. Not to mention the locals

Hate (read Hate) the White Devils from the
mainland—(see Capt. Cook.) Also, one of the to
legalize gay marriages for years!"

Now this was written by someone who should
definitely not live in Hawai'i! Ever! And talk about
creating one's reality . . . as far as we know, there has never
been a hurricane on the Big Island, yet this poor guy
experienced two of them. And volcano eruptions? Well,
yes, our beloved Kilauea has been quietly "erupting" for
some 18 years now. And California has wildfires that
every year do more damage than our volcano has ever
done. Kansas has tornadoes. California also has a
reputation for some not-fun earthquakes. Florida just
experienced four incredibly destructive hurricanes in one
month. Seems wherever you go, Mother Nature has some
tricks up her sleeve.

Anyway, these are admittedly extreme examples of
people who have found what are to them, valid reasons to
get out of the islands as quickly as possible.

One more example from this same magazine and
then I'll quit. I have lots more, though, for those who
might be interested!

"[Other contributors] made good points in their
views of Hawai'i but they didn't mention how
stupid and intrusive the state government is.

"I'd advise anyone who wants to move here to do
his or her homework first. Find out why an ever-
increasing number of the local people are moving

to the continent. Ask why people move back to the mainland after a short residency here. Save yourself some stress and ask first."

Indeed! I certainly agree with the "ask first" part. "Experience first" would be even better.

The reason I'm sharing these vignettes is that they demonstrate how differently each of us perceives the same situation. Other than the presence of continual teensy earthquakes near the volcano and the volcano itself, we have not come close to experiencing any of the trauma of these writers, nor do we know of anyone personally who has.

For sure, we have known folks who came here with stars in their proverbial eyes and in the end went back to the comfort zones of their old environs. They did not make it here. We've known very nice people who said that after a year here they had not been able to make any friends. And then we know of others who seem to be friend magnets; wherever they go they accumulate new friends. And the latter is the way it has always been with us here.

Women seem to be more sensitive to the nuances of Hawai'i's energy. There seems to be no halfway with them; they either love it or do not make it here.

Good Reasons Why NOT to Move to Hawai'i

We've talked about a few of the reasons that so many people turn tail and head back for the Mainland after trying Island life for a while. This all may sound terribly negative to anyone who is enthusiastic about the possibilities of moving to the Islands, and indeed, much of it is. That's why we're talking about it now, so you can get a sense of the "other side of the picture." That's only fair, after all.

Live Aloha Wherever!

One need not live in the Islands to live a life of aloha. Most of us are fortunate enough to know or at least have known somebody who lives aloha, even if it's in downtown Chicago!

Different Place, Same Problems

Many of us who are troubled by one thing or another seem to feel that a change of scenery will somehow fix everything. Maybe it's the hectic pace of city life, family problems, a boss we have trouble relating to, or just some restlessness. Sometimes a change of scenery might be all it takes for us to get ourselves grounded and be able to function at a new level that makes positive changes in our lives.

But too often, we tend to bring the old baggage with us. The new place feels really great for a while . . . while it's still new. Then pretty soon, the things that somehow fascinated us at first start to irritate us and we begin unpacking that old baggage. Before we know it, we're trying—most likely at a subconscious level—to make the new place more like the old place, and soon, the frustration starts all over just like it did before.

It's really important that we seek our new environs for the right reasons. Ideally, we don't do it as an escape, but rather as a move to some place that feels even better than where we are now. Well, that's the ideal way. It's kind of like hooking up with a new partner; if you're coming from an insecure, needy place, you're not likely to be moving into an aspiring new relationship.

We would like to think of your move to Hawai'i as adding a brilliant rainbow to your already beautiful, bright blue sky.

Since it's probably unreasonable to assume that all of us will be in so enviable a space in our lives, let's go to a more likely scene: We're wage-slaves in a big city, making lots of money and spending it faster than we're earning it. We can feel in our hearts the shallow existence of working so hard just to be able to keep paying the bills that let us afford to keep working so we can pay more bills, ad nauseam. We know that there's something better out there; that this is not what we were put here for. Then one day, we decide to take a vacation to Hawai'i, and when we step off the airplane and take our first breath of Hawai'ian air, we just know in all of our being that we have just come home-that this is where we must be.

We spend the next few days nearly overwhelmed with the beauty of everything, and with that magical, mystical feeling that is so pervasive and just makes us want to hug everyone. We breathe that sweet, sensuous air, swim in the caressing, crystal-clear ocean; feast on sumptuous tropical fare, and just drink in the essence. We're hooked!

This is what happens to a lot of folks; it's what happened to us. But if it goes far enough that we start to consider actually relocating to Hawai'i, it's time to feel the lifestyle in its entirety.

A Peaceful Existence . . . Challenged

There are many ingredients to this peaceful existence, and they mostly revolve around a general attitude that people are more important than things, profits or time-tables. A simple example of this is the "talk story" story we told you earlier. You don't even consider saying to your neighbor that you are just on your way out; you invite her in, fix her a cup of coffee and you listen to what she came to tell you, or if it was nothing in particular, you just enjoy the Now of each other's company for awhile. You don't take those periodic Mainland-style glances at your watch. You probably don't even own a watch! In due time, she leaves and you head for your friend's place, arriving some time in the early afternoon. Your friend doesn't ask why you're "late," because outside the realm of business appointments, "late" is kind of a foreign concept here and not often considered.

In personal relationships, this works better than in business arrangements, but it still happens there, too. A contractor might simply not show up for the job he said he'd do, because the surf was particularly good that day

35

and no way was he going to miss it. This is understood here to a certain level and accepted by many. There is a point at which it's not very nice to space out a business commitment, and this is exactly the point where you'll find that those who keep their commitments are the ones who are never looking for work.

The key, of course, is to be at peace with this lifestyle, and if that comes naturally to you and feels very good to you, then at least in that area you'll probably do well here. If it feels like it will take all the patience you can muster to put up with the leisurely ways of the Islands, then this might not be your cup of tea.

This casual attitude is pervasive here, and it's just part of life. It drives some people up the wall, and others fall into a comfortable step with it. It's important to would-be residents that they be honest enough with themselves to know that their acceptance of this kind of lifestyle is real and not just fun because it's new. Folks who have spent a good part of their lives on the Mainland big-city treadmill or living a life of appointments and time-tables might have difficulty adjusting. If you feel uneasy about the adjustment, we strongly suggest renting for a while before making a commitment to live in Hawai'i.

It's a very good idea to allow enough time to know if what you are feeling is real. Lots of newcomers here just love the lifestyle for a while, and indeed it feels good to them to set aside their old mainland frenzy. But too often, after a month or three, there seems to be a need to ramp up the pace a bit. Things are moving just a little too slowly now. What you need to realize is that if you feel that kind of need creeping into your new life in the Islands, it's only going to get worse. Your need to speed things up will not be satisfied until you're back doing the same thing here that you were doing there, only here it won't work. It won't work because you will be encountering constant resistance to your new project: trying to change the pace of Island life to your needs. It hasn't happened yet, and it isn't likely to.

Island culture is a resilient culture, even under all the pressure it has endured for the last hundred or so years. We are thankful for that!

Leaving Behind Family and Friends

Another issue we recommend for serious consideration is that of leaving behind family and friends. We've heard from dozens of families and individuals who put everything they had into moving to Hawai'i, only to return to the Mainland in a year or two because they could not deal with the distance between themselves and their families.

Grandparents seem to have the biggest problem with it. Recently, we were at a garage sale in our little community and met these folks for the first time as they were selling their belongings in preparation for their move back to the Mainland. We asked them why they were moving, and they replied, "We need to be close to our grandbabies."
Sometimes it is grandkids, other times it will be kids, parents, grandparents, or even friends.

We have kids over there, too, and we miss them terribly. But in this mobile society of ours, we could conceivably move back to California to be closer to them just as they decide to move to Florida.

Even as I sit here on our lanai typing away, my Lovely Bride is in California with her daughter and our 16-month-old granddaughter. And in February, there will be another grandbaby born and she will make the trip again. It's really difficult, this distance thing. Not to mention expensive. The bottom line is that we would rather make a few trips to the mainland than to leave this Island.

Funny, I can recall when we had babies and it was always us who traveled the 500 miles to visit their grandparents. That seemed normal in those days. Nowadays, our kids are so insanely busy with their big-city lifestyles that they "just can't get away," so we have to do the traveling if we want to see them.

We've thought long and hard on these issues, and have come to the conclusion that Hawai'i is where we must be for our own peace and happiness. We worked hard for many years to be able to now live our dream; a modest lifestyle in the one place on the planet we love best. It is also our kids' option to live where they choose, and they just happen to choose a different place. We still see them, although not nearly as often as we'd like. Although it wasn't an easy choice, we have made the conscious decision to live with it this way, and always silently hope that at least some of them will eventually join us here.

Other people handle it in different ways. One couple we know moved back a little over a year ago because they felt that need to be closer to their kids and grandkids. After spending the better part of a year back in Oregon learning that their kids had busy, active lives and that they hardly ever had any time to share with their parents, this couple said the heck with this, we're going back! They subsequently made the same decision we did and are here to stay.

We've heard this same story from others, too. After going back, we hear they don't see the kids any more there than they did when they lived here, and furthermore, when they lived here and the kids came to visit, there was more quality time than when the parents tried to fit into the kids' busy schedules on the Mainland.

It isn't always like that, though. Some people simply cannot tolerate such a distance between themselves and loved ones, and it is really important that you take a close look at yourself, your family ties and how well you would do with your family an ocean away. Consider how often you see your kids, your grandkids if you have any yet, parents or other loved ones, and what a difference it would make in all of your lives if you were no longer involved in the same way.

Parents, or even grandparents, present a whole new set of rules, too. With kids, the decision might be a little easier just because everyone involved is mobile. It doesn't take a lot to jet on over to the Islands for a visit. With elderly parents or grandparents, especially those who depend on their families for support in any number of ways, it becomes a different matter.

These are intensely personal issues and need thoughtful, conscious consideration before making plans to relocate to an Island in the middle of the ocean.

If this all sounds like we're now trying to talk you out of living in Hawai'i, please understand that we simply want you to know some of the details that so many before us have had to learn the hard way. Details that weren't even noticed in the newness of life in Paradise, but then for some, metamorphosed into monsters later on. We want you to go into this with your eyes wide open; conscious and aware that this new lifestyle could well be your Paradise, but that it is not for everyone.

One More Challenge

That said, there are other issues about living in the Islands that you need to know about in advance of buying a home, and one is the dog thing. For some reason, dogs are popular in all parts of rural Hawai'i. Actually, saying dogs are popular doesn't begin to describe the problem. Dogs are everywhere. It is not uncommon for people to own four or five dogs. What *is* uncommon is trained dogs.

Even in town, dogs are everywhere. We are currently remodeling a house a few blocks from our home, and there is hardly a minute in the day when there aren't a few dogs going off. Some bark constantly, from morning till night. Funny thing is, very few people seem to care.

We've talked to dog owners whose animals bark day and night and we've asked them what's up with that. "Hey, they're dogs. Dogs bark. That's what dogs do," was our answer.

We have been in places, some right in nice residential parts of Hilo, where a few dogs will go off at one time. This will encourage a few more to go off, and before long, there is a constant din of dogs that might continue for an hour or more. It sounds like you're living in a kennel.

The constant yapping of dogs is, apparently, like background music to some folks.

This problem has become real enough now that it appears on real estate disclosure statements. If you are about to buy a home and there is no mention of nuisance dogs on the disclosure statement, it would be in your best interest to make sure your real estate agent asks the seller if there are any nuisance dogs in the area.

This is just so you will be aware of the possibilities, and we recommend a walk around in any neighborhood you may be contemplating moving into. Best to know before you sign on the line. We talk a little more in Chapter 3 about checking for neighborhood dogs while house-hunting.

The big problem, and one that is extremely difficult to deal with, is when someone moves in next door and immediately ties up their four dogs that start barking and never stop. That's just a chance you have to take.

Only this morning we went to look at a house that was for sale nearby. As we approached the place, the din of at least half a dozen barking dogs was overwhelming. As we drove up in front of this house, we could see two small dogs tied to short chains in the front yard of the adjacent house. They were frantically yapping, jumping and straining against their restraints. These were typical "tie dogs," as they are called here, and their obnoxious noise was "normal" to their owners. They must either enjoy it or else they don't even hear it.

There were more dogs all around this place, and it could have been the most beautiful house on the Island, but we couldn't wait to get turned around and out of there. Those dogs are probably chasing away most everybody who comes to look at the place, and we wonder how anyone could put up with the noise. Some people feel the need for to have these tie dogs and others have to have two or three snarling pit bulls or Rotweillers. It's hard to understand. Perhaps the writers of the "Extreme" stories above could shed some light this?

There are two more common nuisance-noise situations you'll run into all over the Island. Well, there are certainly more than just two, but these are in-your-face enough that they need some space here.

One is, believe it or not, rooster farms. Raising highly bred fighting cocks is a big-money occupation here. There are rooster farms ranging from ten or twenty birds to several hundred. The visual is always the same: A lot, field, or lawn with row after row of tiny a-frame structures. The structures are usually two pieces of plywood, each two or three feet square, leaning together at the top to form an a-frame. These are shelters for the roosters, and there will be one in or near each structure. Each rooster is hobbled to his individual shelter.

These roosters can crow 24/7. Some cease at night, but not all. When you are within a quarter mile of a big rooster farm, the noise is unbelievable.

Often, you'll see a huge rooster farm right by a large and expensive home, giving an idea of the profitability of these ventures. Cock fighting is totally illegal in Hawai'i, but raising the birds and exporting them is not. Of course, the cock fights do go on here as well, and we occasionally read in the paper about one getting raided by the police. The people who run the farms are apparently insensitive to the objectionably noise, and are equally insensitive about how it affects others in the area. And never mind cruelty to animals.

We recently looked at a gorgeous 1-acre lot near our home. It had some improvements, like a leveled house pad and a beautiful rock wall on the street side. The view from the lot was awesome. You could see most of Hilo, the Hilo Bay, and on up the Hamakua coast. We wondered why this lot was still for sale, as the price seemed very reasonable. When we walked onto the lot a bit farther, it all became clear. There was a huge rooster farm about 300 yards away, in plain sight, and even though it was downwind, the noise was still very intrusive. The lot is still for sale.

Tree Frogs

Here's something you probably never expected would be an issue when looking for a home in Hawai'i: Tree Frogs! In case you haven't heard, there has been an invasion of tree frogs all over the Big Island. All over Hawai'i, actually.

East Hawai'i is actually an ideal environment for these tiny creatures, which are about the size of a nickel. So what's all the fuss about? The frogs, also known as "coqui," are very noisy. Their call is hard to describe, save that they were named after the sound they make. It is high pitched, and when there are only a few of them, it could even be described as pleasant. Hundreds of them begin to transcend any definition of "pleasant" and the thousands that are now appearing in many places here are so loud that in some places it is difficult to carry on a conversation.

They have become so common now that their presence must be reported on real estate disclosure statements, and this is exactly why I am posting this report.

The presence of tree frogs is not always reported, as it is up to the seller to fill out the statement and of course, it is to the sellers distinct advantage to "forget" to do so. Since the statement only asks one to report unusual or annoying noises, a seller to whom the din of tree frogs is music might fail to report it as annoying.

So if you are looking at real estate here, it's up to you not only ask, but to check for yourself! You can do this easily by simply going to the property after sundown, better yet after about 8 PM, and listen for yourself. If there is even only one tree frog sounding off, be assured that it is only a matter of time. Actually, the way they are multiplying, it is probably only a matter of time before they are everywhere.

What is being done to control this matter? Not much. The County has known about the problem for several years, but during the initial period when something could have been done easily, the matter was in heated dispute with environmentalists and others sympathetic to the cause of the invaders. Now it has grown to such proportions that eradication, according the latest reports from the County, is impossible. We are told that the best we can hope for is to slow further spreading and perhaps eradicate new, small, fairly isolated populations of them. These invaders are not only a nuisance to those of us who might otherwise enjoy a good night's sleep; they are also a significant threat to Hawai'i's delicate ecosystem.

An example of an eradication effort by the County is the Lava Tree Park project. A crew of workers came in and decimated all of the beautiful tropical undergrowth of a major portion of the park. They removed everything right down to the dirt. Then they sprayed a citric acid solution that is reported to kill the frogs. Trouble is, as they were cutting and whacking, all the little froggies hopped out into the surrounding jungle and as soon as the protective vegetation grows back, they'll hop right back in. A night visit reveals that the frogs are still there, although right now they are not as loud as they were before the "war on frogs."

The frogs are spread in many ways here, and our residents are not helping the matter. Some, we have heard, have actually captured these "cute" little critters and taken them home to what were at that time frog-free areas. Another cause of the spreading are "flower and garden" operations that routinely sell potted plants complete with hitchhiking frogs. It is thought that hitchhiking on imported potted plants is how they arrived here to begin with. Wal-Mart in Hilo has had frogs in their garden shop for some time now and they claim to be telling their employees to "pick the frogs off of their plants," but it isn't working.

So there you have it. The tree frogs are quiet during the day, so don't assume
a frog-free area until you've personally checked it at night. Check nearby as well, because if they are close, they'll be around soon.

For further info on Hawai'i's tree frogs, type "Hawai'i tree frogs" into your favorite search utility. You will be surprised by the amount of data presented there.

And More . . .

Then there are some more things to look for when shopping for rural property, like hog farms that happen to be upwind of where you might be living. Generally, it's a good idea to look (and sniff) around thoroughly for possible nuisances in any area zoned for agriculture. Ask you Realtor, too, because there are lots of areas of the Big Island that appear to be residential but are in fact zoned "Ag." On an "Ag" zoned lot, it is permissible to have just about any kind of agricultural endeavor, including hogs, roosters or whatever else comes to the imagination. The only exception to this is in some of the newer subdivisions where there are "Covenants, Codes & Restrictions" (CC&R's) in place that specifically prohibit certain activities. For example, one such area that we know of will permit horses and cattle, but no hogs. (Ever been downwind of a hog farm? Phew!)

More on Hawai'i's "High Cost of Living"

We cover the recent escalation in housing prices elsewhere, so this is about everything else.

The "high cost of living in Hawai'i" is like most things here—true for some and a myth for others. For us, it's a myth. For sure, the crazy real estate price increases have taken their toll on living expenses, but even so, the current very low interest rates tend to equalize a lot of the overall expenses. In Chapter 6, we go into the details of how and why the myths are still myths. Here, in our discussion on "realities," we'll prepare you for some of the things that do cost more and are difficult to get away from.

Leaving housing costs for elsewhere, the main areas of higher-than-Mainland costs are electricity, car and homeowner's insurance, and some specific grocery items. Gasoline is an issue to some who come here from the few places where it's still cheaper, but most recently-from-the-Mainland folks we've talked to say that prices are not much different from those on the Mainland. On the positive side is that most people drive a lot less here than they do on the Mainland, where long distances are accepted as normal. Even on the Big Island, the drive from Kona to Hilo, on opposite sides of the Island, is about two hours.

Electricity

Unfortunately, we aren't given any choices here. Unless we use solar or some other alternative to buying our power, we will pay the price. Electricity costs over twenty cents per kilowatt-hour in Hawai'i, which is several times the cost of some Mainland areas. California's recent energy problems have put their prices more in line with ours, and this is apparently indicative of the eventual future of electricity prices nation-wide. Certainly that seems to be the trend.

The upside is that unless you live in the mountains, there is no heating required here and air-conditioning is provided by tropical trade winds, so your overall power bill might not be any more than it was on the Mainland. The average monthly residential power bill here is around $100. We have friends who are very frugal and get by with half that figure, but this is the exception. Our bill for a 1900 square foot home averages $125 a month, but much of that is for power tools, computers, an air-conditioned office, and quite a bit of office equipment. We are also not as frugal as we should be with lights!

Solar, by the way, is a viable, if not attractive alternative here. You'll hear lots of stories about how "solar doesn't work," but those stories are almost always based upon observations of so-called solar systems that were assembled by novices from inadequate components. There are many homes in rural areas here where people rely on these underpowered systems. The systems usually consist of up to four solar panels, an inexpensive (read: inefficient) inverter and a few batteries. They always include a noisy, expensive-to-operate gasoline generator to use when the homeowner needs more power than what will run a few light bulbs.

The stories you'll hear usually go something like this: "Yeah, I've been in a few of those solar homes, and all they have are a few dim lights and maybe a couple of 12-volt appliances, and the owners have to constantly fiddle with the system to get it to work."

OK, here's the other side of the story. There are properly built systems in place here that comfortably run an entire house, year 'round, with no need for a backup generator. What's the catch? The catch is that these systems cost in the neighborhood of $20,000. Yes, that's a pile of money, but if you do the math you'll find the payback is pretty good with the high price of electricity here. Plus as you keep getting your power from the sun year after year, the price of electricity keeps going up for everyone else. Solar components, especially the panels themselves, have dropped in price over the last ten years while becoming dramatically more efficient. Not a bad deal in today's world.

Installing a solar system is something that is best done in the design and construction phase of a new home. It is much easier to design a new home for the most efficient use of light and power—and the panels—than it is to retrofit an existing house.

Of course, it is possible to do a retrofit, and we've seen some successful ones. The biggest obstacle is placement of the panels, which is easy when you can position your new home to best advantage, but must often be built on special racks in a retrofit.

The phone book will direct you to a number of qualified solar contractors who will be happy to answer all of the questions specific to your needs.

Insurance

Some people we talk to say that auto insurance premiums here are somewhat higher than Mainland prices, but as with everything else, you just have to shop around. Rates vary a great deal from one company to another, and even from one agent to another. For those over 50 years young, the best rates are through AARP's Hartford connection, which are about the same as mainland rates.

Homeowner's insurance is comparable with Mainland rates except for the "lava-risk" areas. Although it is higher in the lava-risk areas, contrary to some opinions, it is available. You will still hear from some Realtors and others who should know better that it is still not available in these areas, but the fact is, it is. (We have full-coverage homeowner's policies on our vacation rentals and our home, all of which are in Lava Zone 2.) For a time, the only way you could insure a home in Zones 1 or 2 was through an insanely expensive state-supplied policy. This is no longer the case. Again, shopping around is the way to keep the costs down.

There is one catch to the insurance policies available in the Lava Zones 1 and 2. These policies, at least right now, cap at $200,000. So if you have a home worth considerably more than that, you're on your own for anything over that amount. But then this book is all about affordable living, so we can assume that this won't apply.

A note on "lava risk zones." The Big Island is divided up into areas of varying "lava-flow risks." Zones 1 and 2 are the highest, which means that there is at least a theoretical potential for some future lava flows. How you wish to interpret the risk and how it might affect you is up to you. Many folks here seem to all but ignore the implied risks and the building of homes in even the highest-risk areas seems to go on as though there was no risk at all. We have lived in Zones 1 and 2 for years. Although we didn't live in fear of losing our home to a lava flow, we did acknowledge that it could happen. Kind of like earthquakes in California, hurricanes in Florida, wildfires in any forested areas of the country, tornadoes in Kansas and all of the similar risks people live with nearly everywhere. So now we live in Hilo, which the insurance companies seem to feel is safe. About 25 years ago, an eruption brought a lava flow to within a few miles of the city. Go figure. The bottom line: we keep our insurance paid up and then get on with our lives.

One more detail: In the last few years, some lenders have begun to require "hurricane insurance" on all mortgaged homes. Of course, there has never been a hurricane on this Island, but apparently we get to share in the cost of hurricane damage in other areas in the state.

Yet More on High Prices

Chapter 6 goes into detail on shopping techniques to keep costs to a minimum, but there are some grocery items that are just high here and there doesn't seem to be any way around that. Milk is one of them. The usual lowest price for milk is $3.79 a gallon. Eggs run $1.50 and up, and curiously, imported eggs are usually cheaper than the ones from local producers. Other items that are really high are just about any Mainland-imported, packaged, processed foods. If you must include things like Sugar-Coated Crunchy-Munchies breakfast cereal in your diet, you can save some money by buying the huge packages at Costco. If you have a large family and a freezer to match, you can save big by buying most of your groceries from Costco. Of course, the best deals on fresh produce are from the local farmer's markets. This applies to the markets on the Hilo side of the Island, but unfortunately, the ones in the Kona area seem to have adjusted their prices for the tourists.

We still need to go to Kona for our Costco runs, but maybe one day there will be a Hilo-side Costco, as well. We just got our own Home Depot, so anything is possible!

In Hilo, there is also a "Cost-U-Less" store, which we think of as "Costco Lite." They have a lot of the same things to offer at slightly higher prices. The store is a warehouse-type operation like Costco, but a fraction of the size and an inventory accordingly smaller. Still, they do offer substantial savings over normal market prices for many bulk-packaged items.

We don't have a lot of sympathy for the folks who come to us all worked up about having had to pay $8 for a gallon of milk. They could have bought it some place lese for less than half that amount. Shop around!

Pricing in many of the stores here is a curious phenomenon, especially to people used to fairly consistent and logical prices elsewhere. For example, the norm at Safeway in Hilo for milk prices is this: One brand is priced at 2 gallons for $7. Another brand is $7 for one gallon. The same milk as the 2-for-$7 brand is priced at $2.79 for a half-gallon. Shop around and do the math!

Jobs and "Hawai'i's High Unemployment"

Most people who have ever talked to friends about possibly moving to the Islands have heard the stories about how it's nearly impossible to find work here. The reality is that yes, jobs are not abundantly available. According to the local media, things are improving in this area, but it's still difficult for the average person to find a job, particularly if the applicant has no marketable skills.

At this time, Hawai'i is the number one state in low unemployment, so things are definitely looking up in the job market. Just in our local Hilo paper, where there were perhaps a dozen listings in the "Help Wanted" section a year ago, there is now a page (sometimes two) of listings, and there's lots of variety, too. The construction industry is so desperate for help that contractors are offering to train carpenters!

There are hordes of people moving here now, and as with anywhere else, as the population grows, the need for help at all levels increases.

Chapter 7 tells how you can find the right income opportunities to suit your needs. Key here is that jobs are scarce, but there is no shortage of opportunity. Quite the contrary; opportunities abound!

The People, and "That Local Attitude"

Some friends of ours are a family of several cultures. The parents have adopted several mixed-culture children and on the Mainland where they lived years ago, the kids were always taking various forms of harassment for their ethnic diversity. Imagine siblings, black, white and American Indian, all in the same grade-school arena. They moved to Hawai'i when Dad accepted a position at a school in Hilo and their lives changed in a most beautiful way. They found that their differences were no longer noticed! For the first time in their lives together, these kids were accepted for who they were, and the parents had the good fortune to see their children blossom emotionally and spiritually!

The same thing holds true to a great degree between haoles and locals. It's what's in your heart that counts.

We've heard all sorts of stories from folks who have been here on vacation or even lived here for awhile about how "locals all dislike haoles" and how difficult it is for a haole to get anywhere here because of this alleged discrimination. So over the years, we've observed how this seems to work. It feels to us that most of the locals, particularly those of Hawai'ian ancestry, can see auras. They Know immediately if a person in their midst is there in love or if that person has a pre-conceived notion that generates fear or some other negative emotion in themselves. In our experience, this is a place where the old saying, "you get back what you put out" really holds true.

OK, a little while ago, we mentioned that locals are the folks—including haoles—who have lived here most or all of their lives, and now we're talking about locals not liking haoles. Confusing? After you've been here for a while, you will easily know the difference between a local haole and a newcomer haole. It is the newcomer haole who gets into trouble. Actually, it's the newcomer, and s/he doesn't need to be a haole, either. Any race or culture will do. It's that "malihini (newcomer) attitude!"

We've known more than a few folks who fled back to the Mainland mostly because they "couldn't handle the local attitude." Well, our observation has been quite consistent: these people expected that things would happen the way they did "back home," and when they didn't, their exasperation, anger or whatever, came across loud and clear and was met by what they call "that local attitude."

We have a friend who has lived here for about four years. When he first arrived here, we would hear stories from him about his encounters with haole-discrimination. He's a really nice guy in every way, but to this day he still feels that he is being discriminated against for being a haole. Just a few days ago he told me about the problems he was having at one of our local building-materials suppliers, again because "his skin isn't the right color." Coming from this person, who seems to us to be a gentle, intelligent guy, this is difficult to understand. It has to be the energy he puts out—the energy that comes from the reality he created for himself regarding this perceived discrimination. We do a lot of business with this same supplier and have never, ever, experienced anything but friendly, cooperative service from any of the employees there, almost all of whom are locals.

On a few occasions, we observed somebody who would walk into a public office, like maybe at the County Building, with a visible chip on his shoulder going in. The local person who had to deal with this customer might then come across as being less than cooperative, or worse, actively uncooperative. An effective way of guaranteeing the appearance of "that attitude" is to tell the local person you're dealing with, "you guys are sure behind the times and in Texas, we do it this way."

We've gone in to those same public-office folks and instead of walking in and arrogantly demanding that our will be done, we approach with a bit of humility and aloha, and ask for the person's help. We have never been mistreated and have always received what we considered to be respectful, helpful cooperation. Any time we have not been greeted with exemplary performance from someone in the business arena, it has been from their lack of knowledge or experience, not out of any attitude problem. The difference is when we ask for help, we do just that: ask for help. We do not go to someone and demand that they serve us—our way. It really does make a difference.

Lest we come across as boasting how well we get along with the locals, please understand that the vast majority of people here get along with the locals. It is the distinct minority who do not. Most of them don't stay here long, but some live their lives here, "knowing" all the while that they are being discriminated against.

At the risk of being accused of "profiling," we have noticed that a lot of folks from the East Coast have difficulty here, because for some reason, it seems that demanding a service rather than asking for help is more of a trend there. I would respectfully suggest to anyone who feels like that description fits, to work hard on ramping it down a few notches. For those who practice a whole life of this kind of attitude with others, particularly others in "lower stations in life," this could be difficult. For them, I suggest observing how in Hawai'i, the trash collector and his Ph.D. customer relate on equal terms as human beings, each respecting the other's choices in life. For some people not used to this culture, it is awe-inspiring and life-changing to observe – and then become a part of it. To others, the whole concept is disgusting, the thought of treating a garbage man as an equal is just not going to happen. To them, I suggest that living in Hawai'i is not going to work well.

The reason we put so much emphasis on this is because it is worth considering if you are contemplating a life in Hawai'i. Things do work very differently here, and if you are able to love and embrace the Island ways, you will do well. If this sort of difference will be an irritation to you, you will not be happy here.

A recent Hilo bumper sticker sighting: "We don't give a _____ how they do it on the Mainland."

More on "The Attitude"

There is another aspect of "that local attitude" that needs to be addressed, too. As in most places on our planet, there are always the few who can spoil things for many. Sometimes it's as simple as the few who will throw trash out of their cars, spoiling the beautiful scenery for many. Other times, it gets worse and the effect on others can be significant. Some areas of the Island seem to attract more than their share of these people whom we like to refer to as "unconscious." For example, the Lower Puna District has been one of these areas, although there has been significant improvement in the last few years. You need to know that the incidents of drug and alcohol abuse, domestic violence and other crimes are higher in some areas of this district than in most other areas of the Island. The Virtual Tour (Chapter 4) identifies some of these areas.

Even this is changing now that real estate prices are soaring and people are moving here in huge numbers. Here's what's happening, and if there is an up-side to the population explosion, this is it: A lot of crummy homes in areas that used to be predominantly low-cost rentals, are selling and the homes are being remodeled by people who plan on living in them. This process upgrades the whole community, and it is a fact that here, as in most places, those areas that are mostly low-priced rentals are the ones where the trouble seems to be. Those are the places where the petty burglaries, incidents of domestic abuse, drug offenses and other issues worthy of police intervention occur the most.

Even in some of the worst areas, efforts are being made to clean up the problems, and the results of the efforts are usually directly proportional to the willingness of the individual members of the communities to get involved. "Neighborhood Watch" programs have proven to be very effective in maintaining safe, quiet communities. It is necessary for the community at large to send a clear signal that improprieties will not be tolerated.

We have been told by a number of Police Department folks, including the Chief himself, that the Island Way has always been this: The Police tend to "look the other way" at improprieties occurring in any neighborhood where the community seems to condone such activity. This may seem really strange to somebody from the Mainland where the laws are generally enforced no matter where you might live.

Let's try to look at it from the standpoint of an evolving Island culture. Now we're looking at a little community where petty mischief has always been common and tolerated by the residents. The mischief might include minor burglaries, like kids entering a home and helping themselves to sodas and snacks when nobody is home.

Maybe they've even taken a surf board or two. There may be lots of barking dogs—way more than most folks used to living in quiet communities would consider bearable. Perhaps there's also a slightly obnoxious alcoholic and maybe even a family known to be doing drugs. None of these issues is annoying enough to the residents to do anything about, so life goes on and it seems OK to those who live there. This little village has never really been any different and nobody cares.

Then over the years, a few people from the Mainland come over here and find this area so beautiful that they decide to buy a lot, build a house and call it home. After the initial love affair with the new surroundings starts to wear off, the "normal" conduct of this village starts to become the focus of the newcomers, and as a few more arrive from the Mainland, the inevitable unpleasant exchanges between the locals and the newcomers begin. (Again, in our discussions here, "locals" refers to anyone who has lived most or all their lives in the Islands. Locals are of all cultures and races including haole.) The Police get called about "disturbances" that used to be normal life, the Police talk to the locals and try to smooth things over by asking them to make new compromises to their chosen lifestyle, and they try to explain to the newcomers how this all works. The newcomers interpret the explanation as an unwillingness of the Police to respond to their needs. It isn't. It's just the Police being caught between the proverbial rock and a hard place and doing the best they can. As we've said before, this isn't "America," and it isn't for everyone.

Please know that we are in no way trying to make any judgements about anyone else's lifestyle or the manner in which they choose to live.   Just as if we were contemplating moving to a different country anywhere on the planet, the "locals" are our hosts in that country, and it is best if we honor their cultures and lifestyles and either try our best to fit in or seek residence in an area of like-minded souls.

This can be a difficult situation, and we believe it is best handled by checking out any potential areas for your new home very carefully.   Drive, or better yet, walk through the community.   Do it during the day and at night, as well. Before you decide that this will be your new home, see if the area is mostly local, and if it is, you may wish to rethink moving there unless you feel very comfortable with the lifestyle you observe there.

What is normal life in many Island communities may not be what you consider normal wherever you come from. It is easy to observe geographic similarities when house-hunting and overlook the cultural dissimilarities. For example, you might drive into a community that because of its beautiful ocean view and the curvy streets reminds you of a special place you've visited on the Mainland. You still need to keep in focus that this is not the Mainland, but that it is much more like a foreign country in many respects.   No matter how beautiful or even familiar any particular place feels to you, our suggestions is always to become as familiar as possible with any areas of interest to you.

If you still feel this is where you must be, we strongly recommend renting for at least a few months first.   It is quite possible to spend time in some community for a week or two and never be exposed to the very things that will eventually drive you nuts if you lived there.

This Island is so huge and there is so much variety that it is not difficult to find a place where you will be among folks who enjoy a lifestyle much like yours. Just look around, feel each place that calls you, meet some of the people there, go to the stores and get a feel for the local population, and don't be a big rush to settle into one area just because you like the beach there. There's a lot more to it than that!

The Puna District is huge in itself, and since most of the areas needing the greatest vigilance when considering a move are those in the developments with the lowest-cost housing, you are advised to check around for a predominance of rented homes. Some developments are mostly owner-occupied and others are mostly month-to-month rentals. If you can't tell by the outside evidence, ask your Realtor. The outside evidence includes lots of children's toys in the front yards of many of the homes, older and damaged cars, and a general ambiance of neglect. Bed sheets hung as curtains is another good clue. Yes, this is a gross generalization, but it really does apply pretty well to the communities in question. The ones with a lot of rentals generally have the most problems. Again, see Chapter 4 for more specific info.

The Puna District is also one of the most beautiful places on the planet. There are tropical forests, an awesome ocean, bountiful farming land, and any number of other reasons to choose this place as home. Look carefully and thoughtfully, and pick your spot with the clear intention to allow the locals who have been there all their lives to live the way they choose.

Please do not move into an area that has what you consider to be social problems and think that you will be able to "fix" them. Remember that what you consider to be problems might be quite normal and acceptable in another's culture. Find the place where the residents already feel as you do about what a community should be all about.

One caveat about Puna is in order here. If you spend any time on KonaWeb.com, you will no doubt see some talk about staying away from Puna because of all the crime. Well, this usually comes from people who have never lived here and only like to repeat age-old stories about when Puna was indeed the "Old West" of Hawai'i Island. Things have changed, and now when we read the "Arrest Report" in the local paper, most of the problems are from the Kona side. There are burglaries, drug busts, and all sorts of other crimes reported there every day. Last month there were two shootings right on the main street in Kailua Town, and one was a murder. The bottom line on crime in Hawai'i is that since Hawai'i is now a State of the US, the crime is similar in frequency and in nature to any similarly populated area in the country. It is surely sad that the Aloha State cannot miraculously be free of ugliness, but it seems ugliness is part of human nature. The best we can do, in our opinions, is to create a reality for ourselves that does not include crime. We put no attention on those things that we do not wish to draw into our lives, and so far, it's worked really well.

You've Found Your Special Place

Now let's take all of this to the next level. You've found the perfect place: The people are friendly, those you've met are welcoming you, you don't see any overturned cars or rusted out washing machines in the front yards, there are no snarling dogs, no tree frogs (you checked at night), the weather is right, the traffic is light, and the general ambiance of the community feels good.

Now that you have found a place where the people who will be your neighbors are on the same page with you on your ideas of what a community should be like, it's time for that next level, and that next level is you. Are you ready to not only be a good neighbor, but to be a contributing member of your new community? Will you embrace, with a glad heart, the Island Ways we've discussed so far? Are you eager to leave behind those Mainland habits of timetables, deadlines and frenzy? And once you leave them behind, will you be able to leave them for good?

It's all pretty easy for a while. The challenge is to avoid slipping back into the old ways; to remember never to forget why we're here.

Good Beginnings

During your visits to Hawai'i, as you contemplate living here, please try to feel deeply the things that attract you, the nuances that make you feel so good about being here. It is so important to remain mindful about these things because it seems we all tend to forget too easily.

Often, folks come here and are moved by the feelings of aloha they experience everywhere. Maybe it's just a warm smile from a total stranger, a Hawai'ian-style hug instead of a mainland-style handshake, or a gesture such as getting waved into the traffic lane in front of somebody as you wait to leave a downtown driveway on a busy street. But unless these new folks become a part of the aloha community, unless they themselves practice the gestures and habits that moved them to want to live here, they will instead become a part of the Mainland-attitude community that is beginning to dilute the warm and friendly feelings we've been so blessed with.

We feel it is important to our emotional health to take the time for daily reminders of why we're here. Whatever it takes for you, please invest those few moments each day. Sit by the ocean, go for a walk in a rain forest, take in one of the daily spectacular sunsets, breathe deeply the tropical air laced with the aroma of Plumeria. Listen often to the gentle and soothing sounds of Hawai'ian music. Attend some Hawai'ian cultural events, too. We never leave these events without a renewed love for our Island; a heartfelt love, respect and appreciation for the Hawai'ian culture, and a deep feeling of gratitude for the privilege of being able to live here.

Immerse yourself in the company of others who share your appreciation for these awesome Islands. Condition yourself to be conscious of those around you, their needs and their feelings. Reach out to others, give a little here and there. In ways that can only happen in the magical Islands of Hawai'i, it all comes back to you many times over.

This my sound a bit corny, but I would like to share something with you that is very special to me. My bride and I are fortunate enough to live where we have a beautiful view of the ocean and of the Hilo Bay. As I write this, it is early evening, and I'm out on our lanai writing on my laptop. The sky is ablaze with color— brilliant orange to the west and fading into incredible shades of lavender and deep blue over the ocean to the east. The fading light playing on the gentle waves of the bay is awe-inspiring. We are so thankful, every day, for the blessing of being able to live here.

Live Aloha!

Island People

To those of us who live on the Windward side of the Big Island, the people here are our treasure. Hardly a day goes by that we are not reminded of what we feel to be a perfect ambiance of humanity. We love the ethnic and cultural diversity here, and especially the love and respect—the aloha—that goes on among all of the very different people. Where some folks see "scary people," others see friendly, smiling faces. Where some see an attitude, others see love. Different strokes.

These are the kinds of things that any prospective new Hawai'i residents must feel for themselves. The important thing is to be honest about it; honest with yourself. Feel what it feels like to be here among the folks who make their lives happen here; feel the magic, feel the aloha!

For sure, this is a sensitive topic from any angle I try to approach it, so I'll just dive in and say this: If it feels to you that the local folks here are in any way "backwards" or beneath your station in life, then you need to reassess your vision of living in Hawai'i. I've said it before: This is a different culture from Mainland America. The complaints about locals that we hear occasionally from newcomers and even some people who have lived here for a long time are not only hurtful to everyone involved, they're also painfully ignorant.

We hear people complain about locals speaking pidgin. Well, Pidgin is their language. If you went to Paris, would you consider the French as backwards because they speak English with a "foreign" accent? Are you an unusual enough American that you are bilingual? It seems to me that someone who can only speak and understand one language has little room to criticize another person for being bilingual. And that is what it amounts to. Most of the locals who you might hear speaking pidgin to each other can also speak perfect English when they need to talk to us haoles. In my book, that means they're bilingual.

The whole point of this is that if you cannot embrace these beautiful, warm and friendly people with your whole heart, then you would be better off somewhere where you find the locals more acceptable to your standards. Enough said. But I had to say it.

More Realities: Waiting for What You Want Right Now!

Another source of frustration for some folks is not being able to get what you want right when you want it. Since many of the goods sold here are imported (nearly all), you get used to waiting for special-order items and you try to make do with what's available now. And even if you feel it's worth the wait, if there happens to be a storm blowing through the shipping channel between the islands, your treasures might just have to wait for next week's shipment . . . even if it's already a week overdue. Just go to the beach . . . all in good time!

Having to wait on special orders can become a real problem for those in business for themselves. We've heard complaints from contractors who had to let hired help go because materials were not on the job in a timely manner. The solution is to plan ahead. That doesn't always work, of course, because there can be unforeseen circumstances that make a mess out of the best plans in the world. But most of the time, careful planning does go a long way toward eliminating this source of frustration. After a while, you learn to anticipate what items will need to be shipped in and you'll make sure they are there when you need them.

For example, we're planning on adding a deck to a rental house in about a month. We know from experience that some of the hardware items we'll need will have to be ordered from the Mainland, so they are already on their way and we'll have them here in plenty of time.

We blew it when we added a new bathroom to our home last year, though. We figured we could get the shower door assembly locally, and we were wrong. We could find only one place on this Island that fabricates non-standard size shower doors, and they wanted so much money for the job that we ended up waiting four weeks to have one shipped from the Mainland. We could have avoided the wait by getting prices way in advance.

For the average person or family, most of what you'll ever need can be found locally. It's good to learn to avail yourself of what is here and make it work in your life. We consider ourselves fortunate to be living a lifestyle that requires little in the way of material goods. This kind of a lifestyle lends itself well to peace of mind, unencumbered lives and budgets that easily stay under control.

Kids and School

There is a definite "pecking order" among the young males in this society. It seems to start in adolescence and go on through—and sometimes a few years beyond—high school. It can be difficult for teens getting transplanted to an Island school, but then it is in any school anywhere, to a point. Here, the transplants seem to subjected to a "proving" period, and during that time they will get tested in various ways. The kids with their self-confidence intact handle it fine; others don't do so well at first, but they always seem to manage sooner or later.

Our son was 14 when he first enrolled in school here, and for his first few months he often came home telling us that he might just never go back. One particular group of about six local guys were giving him "stink-eye," and threatening to "kick his haole butt" every time they saw him anywhere. He even avoided going to town with us for fear of encountering these kids. Then one day he had had enough, and all on his own he confronted the bunch of them and told them, "You've been talking about kicking my butt all year. Now's your chance—start kicking!" For whatever reason, this is all it took for those kids to never hassle him again. Matter of fact, from that day on they were all like old buddies.

The trick to getting along while still maintaining your own individuality is to hang with the kids with whom you share interests and keep a healthy and heartfelt respect for the choices of those who do not. Their choices are as valid and proper to them as yours are to you. Always keep in mind that you are now living in a land of many cultures, and we each honor the others. That's the Hawai'ian way.

We've heard a lot of different variations on this story from other guys who attended high school here. One haole friend who grew up in Honolulu and went all through school there said that even though he was one of the star performers on the school's football team, he was still tormented by some of the locals all through school. Then after they graduated, it all stopped as if a hassle-switch had been turned off, and they all became fast friends, which they still are—even after another twenty-five years!

Girls get hassled, too, but it seems more prevalent, predictable, and sometimes intense with the guys. We also hear some heartwarming stories about the warm aloha welcomes received by new kids in the schools. It mostly comes down to the self-esteem of the individuals going in.

The Schools

Big Island public schools have had a reputation for being somewhat substandard in scholastic achievement and over-the-top in rowdiness. We don't really have the hard data to refute any of these rumors, and we do hear some of them first-hand ourselves.

We have friends who are teachers, mental-health professionals and counselors at our local high school. They tell us about some of the kids there who don't care about anything besides surfing and getting high. But they also tell us of some of their remarkable kids who are major achievers. At our son's graduation a few years ago, about 60 kids received scholarships. The curriculum is disturbingly easy in what it actually takes to graduate from Hawai'i's schools, and from that point it's not difficult to see why a lot of the young people here have a tough time finding meaningful work when they graduate. The teachers we know of respond enthusiastically to any of their students who seem to be in school to learn (what a concept!), and in spite of the tarnished reputations of some of the schools here, they all produce some outstanding kids. These are the kids whose parents care about them and their education. They are the kids who care about themselves and their futures.

Our son graduated from Pahoa High with the means to land a high-paying job as a computer-network specialist in California's Silicon Valley. We know of kids who graduated with university scholarships and others who just barely made it through. A huge part of the difference seems to originate in the homes of the kids, which isn't too much different from kids and schools anywhere.

The schools seem to be improving, though, as time goes on. Some schools have widely known excellent reputations and parents will make a special effort to find a home in these school districts. If this applies to your situation, ask around and you'll quickly hear all about which schools excel and which do not.

A relatively new bright spot on the horizon of education are the Charter Schools. Here is some info excerpted from Hawai'i's Education Reform Web site:

"Charter schools are independent public schools, designed and operated by educators, parents, community leaders, educational entrepreneurs and others. They are sponsored by designated local or state educational organizations who monitor their quality and integrity, but allow them to operate freed from the traditional bureaucratic and regulatory red tape that hog-ties public schools. Freed from such micromanagement, charter schools design and deliver programs tailored to educational excellence and community needs. Because they are schools of choice, they are held to the highest level of accountability – consumer demand.

Charter schools operate from 3 basic principles:

Accountability: Charter schools are held accountable for how well they educate children in a safe and responsible environment, not for compliance with district and state regulations.

They are judged on how well they meet the student achievement goals established by their charter, and how well they manage the fiscal and operational responsibilities entrusted to them. Charter schools must and do operate lawfully and responsibly, with the highest regard for equity and excellence. If they fail to deliver, they are closed.

Choice: Parents, teachers, community groups, organizations, or individuals interested in creating a better educational opportunity for children can start charter schools. Local and state school boards, colleges and universities, and other community agencies interested in fostering innovation and excellence in schools sponsor them. Students choose to attend, and teachers choose to teach at charter schools.

Autonomy: Charter schools are freed from the traditional bureaucracy and regulations that divert a school's energy and resources toward compliance rather than excellence. Instead of jumping through procedural hoops and over paperwork hurdles, educators can focus on setting and reaching high academic standards for their students.

Charters provide opportunity for better child-centered education. They provide the chance for communities to create the greatest range of educational choices for their children. Operators have the opportunity and the incentive to create schools that provide new and better services to students. And charters, bound only by the high standards they have set for themselves, inspire the rest of the system to work harder and be more responsive to the needs of the children."

For a thorough look at Hawai'i's Charter Schools, please visit their Web site (See Resource Guide).

Crime and Drugs in Hawai'i

Hawai'i doesn't appear to be much different from any other place in the United States when it comes to these issues. Even Paradise has its burglars. And like on the mainland, street drugs are too easily available, and especially to the kids.

There are areas here that seem to have more than their share of crime incidents, and we identify them in Chapter 4.

There are also areas in which any kind of crime is virtually unheard of. We recently moved from a subdivision where we lived for six years. During that time, we never locked a door and always left the keys in our cars. My big shop full of expensive power tools didn't even have a lock. It was a community with an effective "neighborhood watch" program, and it is one of the safest communities on the Island.

The one crime-related issue that bothers us as well as most folks here is that little seems to be done to prevent car break-ins at spots where people regularly gather, like beach parks. There some notorious places here were car break-ins take place almost daily and several times on a bad day. Ahalanui Beach Park near Pohoiki is one of the worst. Kehena Beach is another.

The thieves hide in the bushes and wait for an unsuspecting person or family to park. If the culprits observe anything being stashed in a trunk, they wait until the owners are enjoying the beach and for the opportune moment when there's no activity in the parking lot, and then they make quick work out of prying open the trunk and stealing the contents. These cretins think nothing of doing $1000 worth of damage to a car to steal $20 worth of goods from inside. When these thefts are called in to the police, the attitude upon taking the report seems indifferent, at best. We've never personally heard of an arrest or a recovery of stolen goods in any of these cases. In all fairness to the officers who must deal with it, they have expressed their frustration with a system that does nothing to an arrested and convicted individual to deter his continuing this evidently rewarding practice.

So how do we deal with it? When we go to the beaches or any of the problem places, we take our old pickup and leave the doors unlocked and the windows down. Our vehicles have never been bothered. We've actually heard from folks who had their windows smashed when the doors were unlocked. Nobody ever said the burglars were bright.

These occurrences are not unique to Puna or the Big Island. We've had rental cars broken into on Maui and on Kauai when we left them at tourist places and even at our hotels. It is an unfortunate little dark side of our population here, but one that we feel you should know about. You're not likely to hear about it from the Visitor's Bureau. It's really not much different from any other tourist destination, but we want to expect something better from the Aloha State.

Politics

We shouldn't even venture into this highly charged topic, but we'll go so far as to give you a heads-up. The political scene just about anywhere on this planet is, unfortunately, a tarnished one. It is no different in Hawai'i. Matter of fact, Hawai'i government, at all levels, has long been famous for its well-established good-old-boy systems and its flagrant abuse of the laws, written and implied. Money talks here and the several old, established interests who have forever owned and controlled most of the Islands have the clout to write the laws the rest of us live by and to bend or ignore them as necessary for themselves. Single-interest agendas abound, and politicians regularly make and carry out decisions that are clearly opposed by the large majority of their constituents.

If you like to start your day with the morning paper and you let these kinds of things get to you, you won't be happy here. Because of the small size of the State and its population, political abuses are in your face constantly. Every day our newspapers carry stories that can ruin your morning coffee, if not your whole day. It has been accepted by most people here that Hawai'i is now and always has been run by and for the special interests of the privileged few. Political promises are visibly bought and sold here on a regular basis. Of course, there are always the crusaders and brave souls who put their lives and careers on the line to attempt positive changes, but most of them give up fairly soon.

Elections and questionable campaign contributions from special-interest firms or groups are as shaky as they are anywhere else, but again, because this is a small place and we all get to know our politicians and their records sooner or later, it's all so obvious. Nobody even makes the slightest attempt to hide the nefarious goings on, either.

Again, how do we deal with this personally? We choose to keep ourselves uninvolved from the things we can do nothing about. This is instrumental to our peace of mind. We do make ourselves available to our friends and neighbors, our community and any other individuals and organizations for which we feel we can actually do some good. This is our way of holding onto our peace in Paradise. And of course, we do our part at the Polls.

Driving Habits

Lots of things are done differently here that can eventually add up to major frustration for some folks. Some of them we've covered above. Another one is a certain local driving style! A few curious Island-style habits (traditions?) take some getting used to. Even more than getting used to them, it takes some amount of acceptance of them if you don't want to be annoyed every time you have to drive somewhere.

If you're from most Mainland areas, you're probably used to driving at or maybe a little above the posted speed limits, right? Well, forget that! Here, the "speed limit" is usually established by someone who chooses to drive at the posted *minimum* speed limit, which on a 55-mph road is usually 45 mph. Nobody seems to know why some people choose to drive so slowly here, but they do, and no matter how many cars are lined up behind them, they don't pull over when they have a chance. They don't take the "slow-moving vehicles" right lane seriously, either. Even some of the slow-moving trucks will simply stay in the left lane through the entire length of a passing lane. The solution is to allow yourself plenty of time to get to where you're going and enjoy the always-beautiful scenery along the way.

There are also some driving habits here that can get you killed if you're not ready for them. One is local-style turns off of a highway. Picture this: You're driving along a two-lane highway (most highways in rural Hawai'i are two-lane) and you're approaching a cross road. The highway traffic has the right-of-way, and there are no right or left turn lanes. The guy in front of you slows down, uses no signals, and as he's slowing, he pulls way to the left side of the traffic lane. He's doing this because he's going to turn left at the cross road, right? Wrong! He's pulling to the far left of the lane because he's going to turn right, and he always turns right from the left side of the road.

OK, now lets rewind the tape to where you're behind this guy, again with no signals going, and he pulls way to the right as he approaches the cross road. Yep, you guessed it. He's going to turn left!

Believe it or not, this happens even if there's a wide enough shoulder that somebody could get completely off of the traffic lane to turn right off of a highway. They'll still take the far left side of the traffic lane and stay there until they've slowed nearly to a stop before crossing the shoulder lane to make that right turn.

This is particularly dangerous to those folks who have moved here from a place where it's common practice to pass to the right side of a car that appears to be waiting to make a left turn. Here, that car might just have slowed to the point where it's about to cross the traffic- and shoulder-lanes to make a right turn.

Please don't get the impression that everybody drives like that here! It's just that it happens enough to be potentially dangerous to folks who aren't prepared for it.

Ready for one more? You're driving along on a 55 mph highway and two or three cars in front of you are going 40. After following them for 15 miles you finally get to a passing lane. Whoopee, right? Right. As soon as the second car is in the passing lane, it pulls to the right of the first one and they stay next to each other through the entire lane, so you're still going 40 at the end of it. It is normal here to ignore passing lanes and just keep driving in the fast lane even if you're puttering along at the minimum posted speed. If you do get a chance to pass in a passing lane, you will most likely have to pass to the right. Even police cars pass to the right in passing lanes, ignoring the person who is illegally ignoring the "slow moving vehicles keep right" signs!

Because of the scenic splendor nearly everywhere, driving in rural Hawai'i can be great. Just remember that it isn't like driving in America. Just take your time and be ever watchful, for the unwritten rules of the road here are different from those you are used to.

A Little Aside

The Hawai'i we're talking about is specifically the Big Island, and then mostly the Windward (Hilo) side of the Big Island. A very different energy exists in other places on the Islands, especially in the heavily-touristed locations. Indeed, Honolulu (on Oahu) is in many ways not much different from being in any number of Mainland cities, except for the year 'round wonderful weather and the white sand beaches. But get lost in the city among all those concrete skyscrapers and traffic jams, and it takes a lot of imagination to remember you're in Hawai'i. Lahaina on Maui is a fun place to visit and play, but again, it's fast-paced, a lot of fast-moving tourist energy, and always party time. For sure, there are a lot of people who wouldn't live anywhere else, but that's not what we're about. For one thing, even if we did want to live there, we couldn't afford it! And to us, these places just aren't what Hawai'i is all about. There's the Hawai'i for the tourists and there's the Hawai'i for living. We're about the Hawai'i for living.

We do cover the more-touristy Kona side of the Big Island because there are folks who enjoy the kind of energy they find there and feel good being in it. It's certainly not anything like Honolulu or even Lahaina, but neither is it like the peaceful, quiet Windward side. Our main focus is on the Windward side.

One way to feel what it will be like living here is to avoid the tourist spots, and instead, rent a condo, apartment or small home in a rural area, in a small community or neighborhood somewhere, or even right in town, as long as it's not a tourist town! You'll find lots of vacation rentals available here by private parties. We own and manage several and advertise then on the Internet. We go to great lengths to explain to anyone visiting our Web site that this is not a resort; there are no white sand beaches here, no helicopter tours, no Luaus, and few souvenir shops! We tell folks that we're a 45-minute drive from town and a long way to everywhere else. Still, a few visitors don't get it and come here and then complain about how hard it is to get to all the tourist facilities! The upside is that the other 99% love it!

What we do offer is a taste of life as it is for those of us who live here, work here and raise our kids here. Those of us who wouldn't live anywhere else. We consider this the "real Hawai'i." You can find many such offerings on the Internet as well as in the local papers, so there's rarely any need to stay in an ordinary (expensive) hotel. (Both of the Island's newspapers are on the Internet and the classifieds are available there as well. See the Resource Guide for addresses.)

We're not trying to invalidate the things that Hawai'i offers tourists! We like to visit Kona and yes, even Lahaina, and play tourist from time to time ourselves, and we thoroughly enjoy doing it. And we certainly do appreciate the need for active tourism here! We just don't want to live there. No doubt lots of folks who love the feeling that is pervasive in the tourist areas like being there better than anywhere else. For them, most of the nuts-and-bolts things we talk about here apply, too. Remember, though, that everything costs more in the tourist areas. Everything, including gasoline, housing, groceries—everything It's not fair, especially to those who live there year 'round. It's all about marketing: charge what the traffic will bear.

Togetherness

If you are planning to share your Hawai'i experience with your family—or even a partner, the first step is to establish the move as a joint venture. Lack of togetherness can make or break a move, even to Paradise. Togetherness is probably the most important element for a family or couple contemplating any kind of a change of lifestyle, and moving to an Island in the middle of the ocean will be a change even if you are already living a life of aloha.

We've seen situations in which one partner was fully into coming to Hawai'i and the other was just tolerating it. One partner truly felt the call and Knew this was to be home, and to the other, Hawai'i was just another place. A pleasant place with nice weather, but just another place. Even for a single person contemplating relocating to Hawai'i, if this is just another place, no matter how great the warm weather is, we heartily recommend rethinking the move. Again, Hawai'i has the reputation for being a cruel hostess to those who should not be here, and the evidence is the itinerant population, especially on the busy Kona side.

Our neighbors of several years had moved to Hawai'i from Southern California some eighteen years ago. "Robert" loved it here with all his heart and had talked his wife, "Margie," into the move. Margie was never really happy here, particularly since they lived in a community about a 30-minute drive from town. She was used to being able to walk to shopping and she never did stop talking about how she missed all of her old friends. It took eighteen years, but Margie finally got her way and with much sadness on Robert's part, they returned to Southern California.

If you are a family, it's really important to feel out your kids if you're thinking about relocating here. It's important to do that when relocating just about anywhere, but moving to an Island is a pretty radical commitment in many ways, and it is good to have everybody on the same page. Often, kids will seem to love the idea of "moving to Hawai'i!" at first, telling all their friends and loving to watch them all turn green with envy. But then when the time draws near, they seem to grow cold on the whole idea. One way to help ease into the transition, finances and time allowing, is to make a few trips over during the year or so prior to the move, and let the kids feel their way around. Let your kids take you to the places that interest them. If you have settled on a particular area of the Island, take the kids to the school they would attend and introduce them to some of the staff. Often, a staff member or even a student will take your children on a tour through the school. Our son was 14 when we arrived here and a lovely young local female student spent nearly an hour taking him through the school and introducing him to some of the students and teachers. That intro did wonders for his enthusiasm about enrolling in the school.

The decision to relocate with school-age children is never an easy one. In some cases, it might be better to wait, especially if your kids have only a year or so of high school to complete. But then there are also the kids who would jump at the opportunity to move to Hawai'i, no matter what!

In Conclusion

Hawai'i is not for everyone. Matter of fact, Hawai'i is possibly one of the few places in the country that is so clearly not for everyone. It is said that Hawai'i will reject those who should not inhabit her Islands, and we have known some of her casualties.

It is important to folks contemplating a move to Hawai'i to understand that this is like a different country. The cultures, the lifestyles, the traditions and the basic ways things happen here are all different. And the more rural your lifestyle, the more profound are the differences.

At one extreme, if you lived and worked in Honolulu, you would be well insulated from the differences. But our Paradise is the Big Island, and our biggest "city" is Hilo. Hilo speaks loudly of the differences. Hilo speaks aloha, and those who do not—or cannot—feel this in their hearts will eventually find it difficult to relate here, and in the end will leave. Most won't know exactly why they're leaving—it just won't feel good to be here any longer.

We invite you to do your homework: feel Hawai'i from your heart. Feel what we've shared in this chapter and if any of it makes you uncomfortable, try to find the source of that discomfort.

When you spend time here in Hawai'i and before making the Big Decision, try to feel deeply the things that attract you; the nuances that make you feel so good about being here. It is so important to remain mindful about these things. Many people, it seems, forget too easily.

We see a lot of people who come here and are moved by the feelings of aloha they experience everywhere. It feels so good to be in this energy of aloha, but unless each of us is mindful to stay there in our day-to-day lives, it is just too easy to fall back into our hurried Mainland ways. It's too easy to forget the very reasons we decided we had to live here in Paradise.

We've been seeing it happen in our favorite little city of Hilo. Only a few years ago, most of the drivers were courteous, would always be conscious of the needs of others in a traffic situation and try their best to accommodate. You would never have to wait in a driveway for more than a few seconds before somebody would slow down and wave you in ahead of them.

Random acts of aloha are happening less now, and we feel this is largely due to the new arrivals who are bringing their Mainland driving habits with them. Or maybe they tried for a while to do it the aloha way and have just forgotten why they're here.

Road manners are a very small part of a big picture, but a part in which the results are clear and obvious. We just wish to encourage you to "practice aloha" in your daily lives. If it is in your heart and it comes to you easily, it will become a way of life and you will be at peace here.

Try this: When you're driving along and you see someone up ahead who needs to make a turn or get into the traffic lane, slow down for a moment and wave them in. It's such a small gesture and one that will cost you nothing, but it means a lot to the other person. The best part is that the other person will almost automatically pass on the gesture at his or her next opportunity. And so it goes. It's so easy, hardly ever done on the mainland, but such a huge part of living aloha.

Always Remember that Aloha is Contagious!

Be careful when selecting your place to call home. Be respectful of those whose lifestyles might differ from yours; they are your hosts here. When you find your special place, become a part of the community. Practicing aloha means giving back to the community—giving of yourself. After a while, it becomes a fulfilling part of life here.

How you determine if this Island Paradise is really for you is entirely up to you. To those of us who make these magical Islands our home, Hawai'i is everything the name Paradise implies. We'd like it to be that way for you!

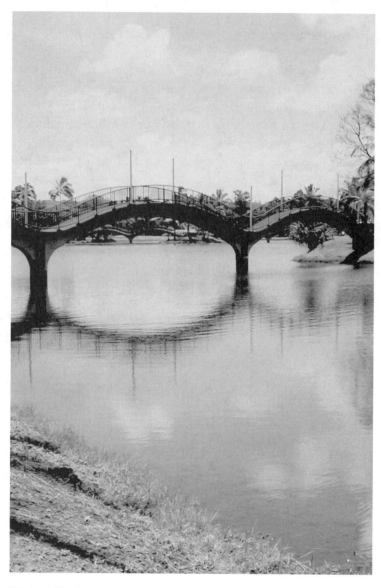

Wailoa Park, Hilo

Chapter Three

Finding Your Own Special Place

Hawai'i has long been famous for its high cost of living. The Big Island, however, has always been the exception and in spite of the recent real estate boom, still is. Sure, there are very expensive homes and other properties here. If you wish, you can spend millions on a home. The good news is that if you're looking for a livable home to buy for under $100,000, you can still find that, too.

We've received quite a bit of flack for the now-outdated housing prices in the first and second editions of this book, but in spite of the all around higher prices, there are still bargains to be had that are simply not available on any of the other Islands. And yes, at this writing (February, '05), you can still find homes for under $100,000. Granted, they will not be in Hilo, nor will they have an ocean view. But if these kinds of prices are what it will take for you to make your move, it's still possible.

More realistically, the prices are now pushing $200,000 for the cheapest homes in any of the better subdivisions, and those subdivisions will be in Puna. The farther you are willing to be from town or from the ocean, the cheaper the land values. Again, this is a generalization, as there are certainly very pricey homes way out of town. But as a rule, the distance from town does govern the prices. We cover more on this later.

The following is a reprint of the latest "Report" published to the ***Affordable Paradise*** Web site. It is relevant to the escalating housing prices.

> We've head Real Estate professionals describe the buying frenzy here as "frightening." And indeed it is, from several perspectives. People are pouring in here from all over the country, most notably from the West Coast, buying up everything in sight. Properties get listed and sold the same day. The day a listing appears on the Multiple Listing Service (MLS), there are usually several over-full-price offers in place within hours. Matter of fact, many properties are sold before their listings actually *appear* on the MLS.
>
> How does that work? Simple. Say you want to sell your Hilo home. You go to the Realtor of your choice, that person takes the info and writes up a listing agreement. Every Realtor has a long list of eager and waiting buyers, so a few calls will bring in the offers, the lowest usually being full price. After the dust settles form the Realtor writing up the offers for her clients, she will eventually get around to the required task of typing the listing in the MLS, even if the property is already sold. That's how it works.

How does this all relate to you as a person looking for that perfect Big Island property? It means that you are wasting your time calling from the Mainland about a property you see advertised somewhere, even on the Internet. If you see it in print somewhere, it's long gone. On the Internet, you might get lucky enough to call before one of the offers already in place is accepted, but probably not.

Don't even bother to ask a Realtor to take your deposit on a property subject to your coming over to inspect the property. No seller will be willing to wait for you when s/he has several full-price offers on the table.

About the only edge you have in this market now is if you are here, you find out about the property the instant it is listed, and you have the cash on hand to make the purchase. By "cash on hand," I do not mean your ability to secure a mortgage. I mean that if you're looking at a $250,000 house, you have $250,000 in cash available—right now—to make the purchase.

Sellers are getting more savvy about the potential problems with purchases that involve mortgages, particularly if the buyer requires a big mortgage. By "big," I mean big compared to the price of the property. When we have a property for sale, we will not accept an offer from anyone who needs more than a 70% mortgage. Sure, there are lots of people out there who can easily qualify to borrow $225,000 on a $250,000 house. Or at least, their credit report says they can. But there's more to it than that. We had one property tied up in escrow for several months while a strong buyer tried working with several lenders to secure a mortgage. In the end, this buyer failed to perform, and we had to start all over again. Fortunately, we had a full-price cash backup offer from the beginning, but that full-price buyer had to wait several anxious months for buyer #1 to drop out. We got lucky; most backup buyers don't have the time or patience for that sort of thing.

Just one of the reasons even a highly qualified buyer might have to drop out after a long time in escrow (this happens all the time) is that the house doesn't appraise for enough to support such a high mortgage. We've also seen a case where the house did appraise for enough, but in the final hours of loan approval (again after months in escrow), the lender went through the paperwork and discovered that there was an addition to the house for which no permit was shown on the County records. So the house had to be re-appraised, and in this market, there's another three-week delay. When it was re-appraised, it came in just low enough that it no longer qualified for the big mortgage. The buyers were not willing to come up with the difference in their down payment, so the deal fell apart.

And so it goes. The bottom line: Cash Talks.

The median home price on the Big Island is now $197,000, meaning that there are still lots of homes available for much less than that figure. But the $100,000-and-under homes are now limited to homes in low-price subdivisions and rural properties, usually far from any town.

This crazy need for so many people to relocate to Hawai'i has caused great difficulty for the folks who live here and have lived here for years. Many of these people have been diligently saving money so that they could buy a home one day. That dream is no longer viable for many of them. The prices of homes in any of the more desirable areas have just about doubled in the last two years. In the really desirable areas, like the best parts of Hilo or Kona, or some of the tourist-destination spots, prices have gone up unbelievably. A little cabin in the once-spurned community of Vacationland that only two or three years ago would have been a hard sell at $75,000 will now bring $250,000 in a heartbeat.

It is our feeling that a lot of these properties are being purchased in the heat of some kind of misdirected emotional charge, and that within a few years they'll be on the market again. People come over here and get all psyched up about "living in Paradise," and they don't take the time of initiative to feel what it is really like living here.

I go through a lot of the realties of Island living in *Affordable Paradise*, and in the near future I'll have another update on some good reasons why NOT to move to Hawai'i.

And one more time, I would like to encourage those who are looking for Hawai'i properties just as investments, to please consider looking elsewhere. Investors do nothing but drive prices up and wonderful people out. Hawai'i is a magical, special place that in our opinions should be reserved for those who feel in their hearts that this is where they must be. [A recent] Issue of **AARP Magazine** has a great article on retiring in Mexico!

The Choices

The median house price here on the Hilo side of the Big Island, *excluding the multi-million dollar properties*, is pushing $200,000. In that range you have a lot of choices, like three- and four-bedroom homes, sometimes on an acre of lush tropical land. Some homes here have "ohanas." Ohana means family, and a real-estate listing showing an ohana has a second home on the property that was supposedly built for extra family, like maybe grand-parents. These second homes are of course also useful as guest homes or even rentals, if the area is zoned to make that legal—and most are.

About now, you're probably thinking something like, "Wait a minute! How come all the statistics I've read say the median house price in Hawai'i is around $350,000?"

In your adventure through this book, you may notice that some of our claims seem optimistic when compared to the statistical reports you've read elsewhere. That's easy to explain. While we insist that it's easy to find an affordable lifestyle here on the Big Island, others will tell you that it still costs 30% more than a comparable lifestyle on the Mainland. They'll back up their claims of high costs of living with "the latest data pulled from all available sources." Well, yes, and from those sources, they're right.

Statistics: You've no doubt heard that old story about statistics: "Statistically, if you have one foot in the oven and the other on ice, you will be comfortable." Statistics can be—and regularly are—used to demonstrate nearly any claim. Sometimes this is done intentionally and other times it may be that this is the only way the researcher knows how to evaluate the situation.

Politicians are notably skilled at manipulating statistics to confirm their positions.

Here's why a lot of available statistics are not viable tools in assessing the information you need. Hawai'i in general, and the Big Island in particular, has a unique set of demographics. Among them: the ratio of very expensive homes to very affordable homes is way different from "average Mainland" figures. In other words, average Mainland statistics will show a far smaller ratio of the total number of homes being in the super-expensive category than here in Hawai'i.

So yes, if you include all the million-dollar-and-up homes in your "Hawai'i home prices" average, that average will go way up. The problem with using these kinds of statistics when figuring Hawai'i's average home prices is that nobody who is seeking affordable homes here is even going to consider million-dollar homes. Or even $500,000 homes! So if you exclude all of the exceptions—the super-expensive homes of which there are many—the remaining average home prices drop substantially. A quick look in the classifieds or in any of the free "Homes & Land" magazines and other real estate publications (available free all over the Islands) will confirm the availability of a big selection of very affordable homes.

Remember, when we quote $200,000 as the median home price, that still means there are cheaper homes as well as more expensive ones.

Just for fun, here are some excerpts from the current issue (Volume 15 Issue 7) of "Homes and Land," a free real estate magazine found in racks all over the Island:

- ❖ HPP 2/1, nicely landscaped, 1 acre, $149K
- ❖ Hawai'ian Shores Recreation Estates, 3/2. New paint, new carpets and flooring, $160K
- ❖ Hawai'ian Shores, 3/2, 15K lot, spacious workshop, $140K
- ❖ Hawai'ian Beaches, 3/1, $115K
- ❖ Hawai'ian Shores lot, 12K sq ft, $28K
- ❖ Country home, 4/2, hardwood floors, $149K
- ❖ Fixer in the hills of Hilo, $125
- ❖ Unpermitted structure on 6 acres in Fern Forest, owner financing, $49K
- ❖ Redwood home, Hawai'ian Shores, 2/2, open beam ceilings, well maintained, $155K
- ❖ Orchidland cottage on 2 acres, no permits, well-built, $97K
- ❖ Kona coffee farm, 7.45 acres, LH, fab views of Kealakekua Bay, $199K

❖ Kona coffee farm, manicured 4.6 acres, great views, LH, $200K

❖ Kona home, 2944 sq ft, $1,695,000

You can see from this list that there are still "affordable" homes available, and some of these appear to be decent places. The last one was included just for fun. Remember to check the **Affordable Paradise** Website from time to time for updates on real estate and other Big Island issues! Check the Resource Guide for the address.

The "Homes & Land" listings are also available on their Web site. Check the Resource Guide for more info.

Also just for fun, here's a little visual in determining average real estate prices. The average price of the homes on the above list, if we **exclude** the last home, is $139,818. Include the last home and the average jumps to $269,416.

To many folks who are from the Mainland looking at homes here on the Big Island for the first time, the prices seem unbelievable. Actually, all of Hawai'i was in a real estate down-market for a long time starting about eight years ago, but things started turning around in about 2001. Then in the last two years, what with the help of articles in huge-circulation money and investment magazines, as well as a mention by Oprah, things have really turned around. All of a sudden, the Big Island is the address to have. Investors and home buyers are swarming in here in huge numbers, buying up everything for sale. Most homes in desirable areas now sell immediately and bring several over-full-price offers the day they're listed.

Many are sold even before their listings show up on the Multiple Listing /service (MLS).

It's definitely still a good time to buy and Big Island prices are not likely to catch up with the other Islands at any time soon, but they are certainly trying. At this point, the prices are still climbing and the general consensus from the professional real estate community is that there is no end in sight.

Many of the sales are to people nearing retirement age. They're buying homes while the prices are still down and of course, the low interest rates make even higher prices seem affordable. Most plan to retire in anywhere from one to five years and they use their homes as rentals in the meanwhile.

To Buy or to Build

Used to be, lots of homes were for sale at prices below what it would cost to replace them. If you found one that you happened to like, it would have made no sense to build your own.

This trend has shifted, however, and in the more desirable areas where prices are still climbing, it is once again worth considering building new. Among the benefits to think about in building new is the fact that wood has a finite lifespan here in the tropics and a new house won't need any immediate repairs for dryrot, termites and other humidity-related problems. And of course, you'll get to design the house you want instead of either settling for what's available or remodeling. An extensive remodel can actually cost as much as building a new house.

It has been our experience that it is easier to find a lot that suits your needs than a finished house. One reason for this is all the people looking for homes right now, most of whom are from the Mainland, don't have the time, patience or skills to deal with having a home built from scratch. The people we talk to who build their own (or have them built) end up with their finished home for considerably less than a comparable home in the same area would have cost.

One item that needs consideration when contemplating building a home right now is that qualified building contractors are in such short supply that they can charge high prices and still not promise that they'll get started on your project for many months. We've talked to a number of people lately who are frustrated by how long it takes to get anything done in the construction field, from getting permits to having the actual building done. Plumbers, electricians, roofers, and all other construction personnel are backlogged for months. And more often than not, we're talking three to six months, not one or two. From this standpoint, buying an existing house sounds attractive, and indeed, this is what's driving the prices way up. Mainland folks come over here and need to make a purchase right now, and they simply go in with higher-than-asking-price offers on many of the listings that come up. You have to be prepared for action to score any good deals in this buying environment.

Another generalization: Building lots range from a low of $4000 to well over $100,000. Lots in some of the bigger subdivisions now go for $25-40,000, and most of these are a full acre. Building lots in and around Hilo go for $90,000 and up. OK, some folks will jump on these figures and tell me about lots priced at $300,000 and up. Well, yes, there are actually lots priced at $1 million and up, if you want to get really ridiculous. But again, we're addressing people who are looking for something affordable, so we're talking about what is available, not how much one could spend.

There's a huge variety of climates, geographical features and flora on this Island. The Big Island has all but one of this planet's weather systems (Arctic), so you may choose from dense, low-elevation tropical forest where it's nearly always warm and humid; higher- elevation forest where it's cooler and drier; high-mountain desert with lots of dry grass and cactus (really!); right at the ocean's edge where it rains little and is always warm, or low-elevation leeward-side where it hardly rains at all.

Fee Simple, Leasehold and More

As you peruse the ads for homes in the two Big Island newspapers or any of the free "homes for sale" publications available all over the Island, you'll come across some terminology that might be confusing. Terms like Fee Simple, FEE, LH, HPP, HOVE and ohana. Let's take a quick look at those.

FS, Fee or Fee Simple means that the title to a property is clear and free from any leasehold encumbrances. The great majority of properties for sale on the Island are fee simple.

LH, or Leasehold, means that the building is owned free-and-clear but the land it sits upon is on a long-term lease. This doesn't really apply much any more, as most of the old leases have run out. There are still a few out there, especially on the Kona side, so we'll briefly explain. Since the few leases that are still in effect are likely to be near their expiration date, it is very important that you look at all the numbers. Many of the existing leases will show temptingly cheap annual or monthly payments, but be warned that when these leases come up for renegotiation, the lessors have routinely raised the rates by as much as 1000%. (That's one thousand—not a typo!)

Here's a typical example. We had a condo in Kailua-Kona, and the lease payments were an easy-to-manage $190 semi-annually. When the lease was close to its renegotiation lease date, the lessor sent out letters to the owners of each unit in the building. We now had the choice of continuing with the lease, with a new "adjusted" rate of $2,400 per year, or we could buy out the lessor's interest in that unit for $40,000. Not much of a choice, was it? We got lucky and sold the condo to someone who was willing to pay the $40,000. (As it turned out, that buyer has more than doubled his investment since he bought the unit from us.)

The bottom line: If you get tempted by a low price on a LH property, make certain that you know the renegotiation date of the lease and whether the lessor has given out the new rates. If no new rates are available, you can use the above example as a guideline. It's fairly typical, according to the real-estate people we've talked to. As a rule of thumb, you can figure that the cost of converting a leasehold property to a fee-simple property will be close to the difference between what the LH property is worth and what a similar Fee-Simple property is worth. For example, if you find a LH one-bedroom, ocean-front condo for $170,000 and the very similar, Fee Simple, ocean-front, one-bedroom condos in the building down the street are selling for $210,000, the Fee-Simple conversion will probably cost about $40,000.

If you are looking at a property where the status of the title is not clearly shown, be sure to ask.

HPP is the common name (and the abbreviation) for Hawai'ian Paradise Park, a huge subdivision about ten miles south of Hilo. HOVE is Hawai'ian Ocean View Estates, an even larger subdivision near the southernmost point of the Island. (These subdivisions are described in the Virtual Tour, Chapter 4.)

We cover "ohana" elsewhere, but for this discussion it is simply the Hawai'ian word for family, and in the real-estate ad context it means that there is either an apartment or a second home on the property. Technically, a second "living unit" is any livable area, even a studio-sized apartment, that includes a kitchen. If the ad says "legal ohana," it means that the second living unit was permitted. If it doesn't say "legal," the second home or apartment may indeed have been legally built for family many years ago, but whether or not it could be used legally as a second home now is questionable. There are lots of these on the Island. Depending on what you would like to use the second home for, be sure to make any purchase offers conditional to the permitted use you intend.

Owner-Built Homes

You'll find quite a few owner-built homes here, and they can be either bargains or nightmares. A few of the considerations when looking over an owner-built home are whether or not the construction was done with a permit, whether or not the permit was ever signed off when the home was finished, and most importantly, the quality of the construction.

If a house was built with permits, you can at least be reasonably sure that the construction was up to code standards (at the time of construction). If there was no permit and you're still interested in the place, you need to look it over very carefully for construction and design flaws. If you aren't familiar with these concepts, you'd be way ahead to have somebody knowledgeable go with you to examine the structure.

Just because there was no permit is not, however, a good reason to reject a home! People do build without permits, especially in the more remote areas, and their workmanship often far surpasses that of most commercial builders. In this case, you might just score a bargain on the home because there are no permits, as that makes the place harder to sell.

One reason it's harder to sell a home with no permits is that it's difficult to get lenders to fund loans on unpermitted buildings. This is also why you'll see some very nice homes here with "seller financing" available. This can be a real bonus for the buyer, because seller financing involves a whole lot less red tape than going through a conventional lender, plus you don't need to qualify for the lenders' sometimes-way-too-strict rules.

Contrary to popular opinion, there are lenders who will fund loans on unpermitted buildings, though, so if you get a "no" from one, keep trying. The considerations here are how well the property appraises and the loan-to-value ratio. In other words, if you have a substantial down payment, you are far more likely to get a loan on an unpermitted building, or one that has an unpermitted addition or two. Be aware that some lenders will not only refuse a loan on anything unpermitted, but they will try to make you believe that this is standard policy among all lenders. Don't believe it.

Some lenders will loan only on the value of the permitted portion of the building. An example would be a home that was built with all the necessary permits but had a lanai added later with no permit. The appraiser will be instructed to appraise only the permitted portion of the home and to ignore the unpermitted lanai.

The reality of this situation is that even though the appraiser is not allowed to count the square-foot area of that unpermitted lanai, it still adds value to the home, and that value does ultimately show up in the appraisal.

While we're talking about permits, another detail worth mentioning is that just because a building has been permitted and the permit has been signed off, is no guarantee that the building was built within the legal set-backs on the property. Strange as that might seem, it is a fact and this is one good reason to have a survey done on any property you get serious about. More on this later.

One more thing about permits, just because a house has all the "proper permits" and they have all been signed off, do not assume that this means the house is well built, or even built to code. Above, I said that you can be "reasonably sure" that the house was built to whatever building code was in effect at the time of construction. Well, the caveat here is "reasonably sure," because we've seen some incredible, flagrant code violations in homes that had been permitted and signed off. How is that possible? We haven't a clue, but it does happen. We're living in a beautifully built older home that was designed and built by a firm famous for its high-quality homes back in the fifties. Well, when we bought it, it had been vandalized and the work of the vandal meant we had to install new light switches throughout the house. The wiring code-transgressions we uncovered were not only startling, they were also extremely dangerous.

We've seen permitted houses built on such substandard footings that the house had obviously already received repairs and retrofits because of the footings sliding down the hill, and they were shaky again. There were poorly repaired cracks in all of the places one would look, considering the movement of the structure.

I could go on with more examples, but the point is simple: If you do not have the expertise to assess these kinds of things yourself, please hire a professional home inspector or at least get a knowledgeable friend to help. By "knowledgeable," I mean somebody who is in or has worked in the building trade and knows what s/he is doing, not somebody who just talks like they know what they're doing. This is especially important if the home you're looking at sits on a slope, near the ocean, or in any way appears to be precarious.

Financing

Seller financing is a bonus for self-employed folks, because they're in the group that is the least likely to be able to get conventional financing. Some sellers would rather have the monthly payments (and the interest!) than a lump sum of money to put into a savings account that pays almost no interest these days. Seller financing also sidesteps the huge loan fees that all of the banks and mortgage brokers charge. This amounts to around $5000 on a $100,000 mortgage.

We occasionally hear from people trying to buy homes who tell us it's nearly impossible to get financing here unless you have a straight job and a sizable, dependable and documentable income. Not so. Several lenders and loan brokers here will finance just about anything as long as the numbers work. Quite a few Island mortgage brokers make "no-doc," "low-doc" or "stated income" loans. With these, there is little or no requirement to show any income or financial statements. The loan is made strictly on the strength of the value-to-loan ratio. This is good for folks who, for example, want to buy an income property and know that their financial planning is sound and that the property will pay for itself, but can't get a conventional bank loan because they are self-employed or retired. If you would like options other than the ones we list in the Resource Guide, ask your Realtor for a lender who makes "no-doc" loans. And as with everything else in Hawai'i, if your Realtor looks at you as if you were nuts and says there is no such lender, just smile and say "Thank you!" and then go ask somebody else!

There is one catch (isn't there always?) to getting these loans, and that is you must have an excellent credit record. You can research this yourself with any or the three major credit-reporting agencies easily found on the Internet). Your "credit score" needs to be 7 or higher to qualify for most kinds of stated income loans.

Today, most fairly-priced homes in good locations sell quickly at their asking prices, or higher. Sometimes much higher. If you're looking for a real deal, seek out the exception: a real junker (but with terrific possibilities) in a good neighborhood, or the very nice owner-built-without-permits home that is hard to sell because a bank won't loan on it. Ask your Realtor to give you a list of homes that have been on the market for a month or more. Also, try to find one Realtor who you can work with and who will be your representative as the buyer. Unfortunately, in today's market, the homes that have been for sale for a while are usually still for sale for a good reason. Mostly they're way overpriced, sometimes they're right on busy streets or in terrible neighborhoods.

A note on putting in those higher-than-asking-price offers; many savvy sellers will now turn down those offers if they are not supported by a notation on the offer agreement that there will be a substantial down payment, like at least 30% of the sales price. The reason is that often, after weeks of tying up the sale of the property to a buyer who needs a 90% mortgage, when it comes time for the appraisal, the house will not appraise for the higher price and then the mortgage will not work, and the deal unwinds. A seller with two offers on the table, one for more money and 10% down and the other for less money but with 30% down, will likely accept the lower offer just because it has a much better chance of actually closing.

Why Some Homes Don't Sell

There's a number of reasons why some properties seem to stay "available" too long, and before you jump in thinking you've discovered a deal that everyone else missed, be careful!

Some homes fail to sell because of tree frogs in the area. Some remain unsold because of rooster farms or other local nuisances. We looked at a beautiful old home in Hilo a few weeks ago that had been on the market for a week already at what seemed to be a reasonable price. The house was in excellent condition, had been completely rewired, re-plumbed and otherwise brought up to current building-code requirements. But there it was, still available. We spent quite a bit of time in this place trying to figure out what made us feel uneasy there, and it turned out to be the view of a very dilapidated home next door that was visible through several windows, but the clincher was the cemetery visible through all of the back windows, the kitchen and dining room. It wasn't right there in your face, but it was clearly visible through the trees and brush. It was an old cemetery, like out of a creepy movie. Now this probably wouldn't bother some folks, but it bothered us and evidently it bothered others as well, since this beautiful old home was still for sale.

The point here is to be careful, spend some time at a potential purchase, and really FEEL the place. Honor your feelings. If you are a couple, honor each other's feelings. My Bride and I have a long-standing deal between us. Either of us can veto a purchase based on nothing more than our individual feelings. We have learned, sometimes painfully, that this has to be.

If you're working with an owner-seller (rather than with a Realtor), be sure to ask for a disclosure statement, and then have a title company do the paperwork for you. It doesn't cost that much, and it is a lot safer than buying real estate with a simple contract between buyer and seller. Often a deal goes through smooth as silk, but sometimes there are glitches that the title company will catch with their routine procedure that could become major hassles down the road if left undetected. This is especially important with rural properties as opposed to those in subdivisions, but it even applies there.

A few years ago, we sold a home in an established subdivision only to discover that the buyer's survey disclosed that the house was built about a foot into the setback! (A "setback" is the distance a building is required to be "set back" from a property line. Setbacks vary from location to location and differ between front, side and rear property lines.) We did not do a survey when we bought this house because the seller was a Realtor as well as a builder and we made some invalid assumptions!

You have two options when it comes to finding the true boundaries of the property you're looking to buy. One is a full survey, which can get expensive. The other is to hire a "pin finder" to find the existing property pins (the permanent corner markers of the property, put there by a previous survey). If you are looking at a rural property, especially one that has irregular boundaries, you should definitely order a survey. In most sales through Realtors, this is required anyway, and the seller usually pays for it.

Here's an example of why a survey is more thorough than a simple pin location. A few years ago, we bought a little house to use as a vacation rental. Had we hired a pin finder, he would have found the pins that were clearly visible at what appeared to be the lot corners, and that would have been the extent of his responsibility. A survey, however, brought a crew who had the latest Platt map, which clearly showed a conflict between the pin locations and where the lot lines should have been. It turns out that the previous owner of this property and the adjacent lot had had the boundary line moved several years ago. The reason was that he had intended to build his home on the adjacent lot and the boundary-line move gave him an extra ten feet by taking the ten feet from the lot our little house was on. The surveyors, with some extra diligence, found an additional and barely-visible set of pins defining the new lot line. Had we relied on a pin finder, this sale would have gone on record with the wrong lot dimensions.

Simply having the wrong lot dimensions recorded with the sale of the house would not be a big deal in itself, but what if we would have decided to add onto the house and build that addition right up to the setback of that incorrect property line? The building department most likely would not have caught the error when they issued us a building permit, but maybe the adjacent lot owner would have complained about the intrusion onto his property, which could conceivably start a long, drawn out legal procedure and even force the removal of the addition.

One trick worth mentioning is that if you are considering a subdivision property and no survey is required in the purchase but you would like to know where the property lines are, look at the adjacent several lots to see if there has been a recent survey done. You're looking for a stake with a colored ribbon tied to it, or a pipe driven into the ground. If you find pins on an adjacent lot, you can find the pins on your lot by measuring from the existing pins. Of course you will need a plot plan with measurements, or even a plot map of the area, some of which have lot measurements. If there's no plot plan available, use the dimensions on the Realtor's listing agreement. Measure the lot on which you found the pins, and if it is of the same dimensions as those shown for your lot, it is reasonably safe to assume that all of the lots are the same size. "Reasonably safe," by the way, means it's OK to use this method to find lot boundaries when you're looking at a property, but it is not safe enough to rely on as the last word in the final purchase.

It's best to do what you can to be sure of your boundaries. In Hawai'i it's also smart to ask for a termite report, and if you don't feel competent to make a thorough inspection of the property yourself, hire a home inspector to do it for you. Again, hiring a Title and Escrow service to do the paperwork for you will make sure that all bases are covered. Even if you can handle real-estate transactions on your own, there's high probability that Hawai'i requires documents or procedures that your home state did not, and it is best for all parties concerned to do it right the first time. The cost is insignificant in the big picture. See the Resource Guide for a recommendation.

It is also important to know that dryrot is a bigger problem in many areas that termite damage, and a termite inspection generally ignores dryrot. The report will mention only termite (or other insect) damage. Again, if you do not feel qualified to do these inspections yourself, please hire a competent home inspector. We have listed one with whom we are familiar in the Resource Guide.

A note here on the pros and cons of hiring a Realtor . . . Most Realtors are quick to tell you how essential their services are and how much more smoothly transactions go with their help. For us and for others we know, this has clearly not been the case. Especially in this busy market, many Realtors are so busy that it is a real stretch to give each of their clients the time they deserve, particularly when transactions require out-of-the-ordinary services. We've been involved in these kinds of transactions, as with the purchase of a bank repossession, and the paperwork became insane. In one, we ended up doing about 80% of the legwork in making all the necessary phone calls to keep the transaction moving forward, and in the end it still took five months to complete and ended up costing thousands more than the original sale price of the house. Our Realtor was so confused with all the goings on of this deal that there were mistakes made; contacts between attorneys, title company agents, sellers and us forgotten; faxes misplaced; ad nauseam.

Yes, sometimes it can be easier to use a Realtor, as long as the deal goes smoothly and your Realtor is up to speed with the "new rules" of wheeling and dealing in this frenzied market. We know of a few in this category, but still have consistently better results on our own. The transactions always seem to go smoother with far less paperwork when we buy or sell on our own.

Here's the deal. Mostly, once a buyer and seller of a particular property have been identified, all the Realtor has to do is to make out the original Deposit Receipt and Offer Acknowledgement (DROA), get the seller to complete a disclosure statement, and then take those documents to a title and escrow company. From that point on, the title and escrow company does everything else. Sure, if there's a glitch, the title company agent will call your Realtor to tell you about the glitch, but if there was no Realtor in the loop, that same title company agent would tell you directly. It has been our experience that eliminating the extra person in the transaction also eliminates a lot of possibilities for inaccurate interpretations between other agents, sellers, buyers, and others. Of course, another job of the Realtor is to make sure that the buyer and seller never talk to each other directly. Again, we find that dealing directly between buyers and sellers makes for a smoother, more reliable transaction. This has just been our personal experience.

One more thing, that six percent commission can make the difference between a purchase being a good deal and not. A house that must bring to the seller $200,000 has to sell for an extra $12,000 to pay the commission. Back when it was hard to sell a house, it might have been a great deal to pay that huge commission to find a buyer, but in today's market when most homes are sold the day they're listed, that commission feels pretty pricey.

Another detail worth mentioning is that you, as a buyer, will have a distinct advantage if you work with the selling agent as opposed to working through an agent of your own. The reason is simple. A seller's agent is inclined to steer his or her client to an offer that comes in directly instead of through a buyer's agent. I'm not suggesting that the seller's agent would do anything to violate his or her fiduciary trust with the client, but let's assume for a moment that your offer and another have come in at the same time. The offers are nearly identical, would net the seller the same amount of money, but one offer came in directly and the other through another agent. If the seller accepts the offer that came in through another agent, the seller's agent must split the commission. An offer that came in directly from the buyer nets the seller's agent the full commission. We feel we have lost at least two very promising deals because we had our agent present the offers. Never again!

Free Information

Once you find a house or piece of land you're interested in, it could be to your advantage to know some history about it. See the Resource Guide for the Web addresses of Hawai'i Information Service and the County Records for the hot setup to find out just about anything you would like to know about a potential purchase.

If you do not have Internet access, the tax office in Hilo will let you use their computer to look up any piece of real estate. All you need to know is the Tax Map Key, or "TMK." This is the number that identifies that particular parcel of land exactly, and it will be on any listing agreement or form that you get from Realtors describing a property they are showing you. If that isn't available and it's important to you to look up the info, you can consult the area maps available at the public library and find the TMK yourself. Most Realtors also have these TMK maps in their offices and will let you look up a specific parcel. When you're still at the property, make note of any landmarks at or near the lot in question, like how many lots from the corner of what streets. That will make it easier for you to locate the correct parcel on the map.

The public documents at the tax office (available to you either at the office or on your own computer) consist of a history of current and previous owners, a description of the parcel, what its land and structure assessments are and have been over the years, any sales and the dollar amounts of those sales. The amount and date of the last sale of a parcel can be valuable bargaining information for you when buying a place.

If a parcel or home has been sold every few years over the last ten, it would be a good idea to find out why. If the current owner has only had it for a year or less, why is it being sold again? If the current owner recently bought it for half of what he's trying to sell it for now, is he in the business of buying and selling for profit? These and other considerations can all be of use when coming up with an offer. See the Resource Guide for the addresses and phone numbers of the County Office and the Library and the County Records Web address.

In Conclusion . . .

Don't listen to all those "statistical reports" on how expensive it is to live in Hawai'i! Check it out for yourself, and you will be pleasantly surprised. You can do a lot of preliminary checking on the many Hawai'i real estate Web sites. Just type "Hawai'i real estate" into your browser and click your way to the Big Island. Check the Resource Guide for some specific Web addresses.

We mentioned before that if you choose to work with a Realtor, try finding one with whom you can enjoy working and who will be your representative as the buyer. Remember also, if you go to the listing Realtor, s/he is the seller's representative and has the seller's best interests in mind at all times. It is clearly to your advantage to use the services of a Realtor who has your best interests in mind! If you continue to work with the same buyer's agent, that person should, after a short while, know exactly what you are looking for. If s/he continues to show you places that you have no interest in, find a different Realtor! Better yet, find the places you're interested in on the Internet and then call the listing agent!

On The Big Island, you can find anything from a grass shack to a fantastic ocean-front home; any kind of climate from desert-dry to rain-forest; you can be in town or as rural as you like; live in a subdivision or have your very own farm. And the best part is that compared to most other places where one would really like to live, it's still affordable!

Hawai'i Island

Driving distances

Hilo to Kailua Town by way of Kamuela: 100 miles
Hilo to Kamuela: 59 miles
Kailua Town to Na'alehu: 57 miles
Hilo to Na'alehu: 55 miles
Kamuela to Hawi: 21 miles

Chapter Four

The Virtual Island Tour

Now let's take a tour of the entire Island. We'll stop in each community and take a good look around, so you'll have a basic idea of what to expect. With this information you should be able to narrow your search to a few possibilities instead of spending weeks on an actual tour. At the very least, you'll be able to eliminate places that get really cold if you like to stay warm, homes up in the mountains if beaches are important to you, or places that are an hour's drive from town if you'll need to commute.

Note: The exact locations of every community and subdivision can be found in the East Hawai'i and West Hawai'i Guide Books mentioned in the Resource Guide. We highly recommend you have the appropriate book with you on your tours.

Our itinerary starts in Hilo and goes around the Island in a clockwise direction (assuming you're looking at a map).

This will be our around-the-Island itinerary. The indented names are subdivisions and small communities.

Hilo
Kea'au
HPP
Orchidland
Ainaloa
Hawai'ian Beaches
Hawai'ian ParksHawai'ian ShoresNanawale
Pahoa
Kapoho
Leilani Estates
Red Road area
Kehena Beach Estates
Kalapana Seaview
Puna Palisades
Kurtistown
Mountain View
Glenwood
Fern Forest Estates
Fern Acres (a.k.a. Crescent Acres)
Hawai'ian Acres
Volcano
Wood Valley
Pahala
Na'alehu
HOVE (Hawai'an Ocean View Estates)
Honaunau
Captain Cook
Kealakekua
Holualoa
Kailua-Kona
  Subdivisions close-in to Kailua Village

> Subdivisions north (toward airport) of Kailua
> Village

Kawaihae
Hawi
Kapa'au
Waimea (Kamuela)
Honoka'a
Laupahoehoe
Honomu
Papa'ikoa
Back to Hilo

The Virtual Tour

Our tour begins and ends in Hilo. We'll cover each stop on the tour with a general description of the community, the weather, the ambiance, and any noteworthy things you need to know. If any of the places we visit have special reputations, such as beauty, safety, serenity, or even crime, we'll let you know.

Let's look at some factors common to many of the areas so we won't have to repeat the same info for each place. First, the terms "mauka" and "makai." In Hawai'i, we use a unique system to describe direction. Since all the Islands are basically round(ish) and the main roads go around the outside of the Islands, the usual terms of north, south, east and west are difficult to apply here. So we use mauka and makai.

Mauka means toward the mountain. You can remember it by the phonetic association of mauka and MAUntain. Makai means toward the ocean. Kai is the Hawai'ian word for ocean. Actually, anywhere you find yourself, it's almost always easy to tell which way is mauka and which is makai. Usually, mauka is the uphill direction and makai is the downhill direction. After a while, it becomes quite natural and you always know where the ocean is relative to where you are at the time.

Another term you'll see on our tour is "catchment system." Many of the homes here, even those in large developments, rely on rainwater catchment systems for their domestic water needs. On the Windward (Hilo) side of the Island, this works well because there is usually enough rain to keep the system well supplied. These systems consist of a metal roof on the house, rain gutters with pipes directing the water into a large (usually 6-10,000 gallon) tank, and then a pressure tank and pump just like on a system that uses a well. Properly designed and constructed catchment systems are very reliable and the water, usually run through one or more filters, is great. It's soft, mineral-free and tastes wonderful. Some people don't drink their catchment water, but most do. We did for years and prefer it by a wide margin to any municipal water we've ever tasted.

Some of the homes in remote areas have solar electrical systems, too. There are whole subdivisions that have only recently had municipal power run in, and with much controversy at that. A lot of the people who had well-working solar systems didn't want the ugly utility poles and wires in their views, while others who had inefficient or substandard systems welcomed the utility into the neighborhood. The power company fought hard to preserve their "right" to install their poles and wires anywhere they wanted to, and as usual, the big guys won.

One last thing before we begin our tour. As you drive through the communities of the Big Island, you might wonder why so many homes appear to be built up on stilts. The reason is to catch breezes! Especially if the home is in a forest, or even if there are trees or shrubs around that would block the prevailing tradewinds from the building, a house built on stilts will be much cooler and more comfortable inside when it's up high enough that the breezes come through. It's as simple as that. When you see houses near the ocean built way up high, it's because of the new building regulations requiring any home within range of high-tide or winter-storm ocean waves to be built that high. Some of them seem really ridiculous built as high as they are, especially when they're right between two other homes built right on the ground. The two other ones were built before the experts decided on the new rules, and some of them have survived 50 or more years of winter storms without ever getting wet. Go figure.

OK, here we go! Our first stop will be the beautiful city of Hilo.

Hilo

Hilo is our favorite little city in the world. Hilo is, to us, the essence of aloha! The people are gentle and friendly, and life moves at a pace that's comfortable and easy-going. Hilo is rich in the heritage of these islands, and it shows in daily life here as well as in the varied and frequent cultural events.

Hilo is a city of parks. The highway running along the edge of beautiful Hilo Bay is lined with parks on both sides. Often, you'll see kids' soccer games or other sports activities going on there, and there are picnic areas and even a pavilion in which you can enjoy all sorts of musical events. Along the waterfront at Hilo Bay are canoe sheds filled with the exotic craft used by canoe clubs and cultural events.

Liliuokalani Gardens is a formal Japanese garden park off of scenic Banyan Drive. There are small bridges over quiet ponds, pagodas, stone lanterns, and an ambiance that is distinctly inviting. Nearby is Coconut Island, yet another park and this one is accessible by footbridge. This small island is the home to some unique

Liliuokalani Gardens on the Hilo waterfront

Hawai'ian cultural events and is commonly used for weddings and other gatherings. The cover photo on this book was taken from Coconut Island. All of these places

122

provide a very relaxing atmosphere for a day's meandering.

Banyan Drive is where most of Hilo's hotels are located, and the drive is worthwhile even if you're not looking for lodging! Alongside the curving road are huge banyan trees, planted many years ago by celebrities like Richard Nixon, Amelia Earhart, and others. Their names appear on plaques at the foot of each tree. At one end of the drive is an inlet from the Bay where many small sailing boats are moored. There's a small white sand beach there, too, and hardly ever more than a few people!

If you're not yet tired of parks, drive out Kalanianaole Avenue about four miles to the end, and all along that ride you'll see the most inviting small parks on the ocean side of the road. In many, you'll see children playing in the shallow, crystal-clear tide-pools, while the older and more adventuresome are out playing in the surf beyond. Picnic areas, pavilions and other park facilities seem to be everywhere along this beautiful drive. Near the end of the road is Richardson Beach Park, and here it's definitely worth your while to get out of your car and take a walk. The ocean vistas are awesome, and the park itself is friendly and beautiful. The accessibility of all these wonderful places is just another reason why Hilo is a great place to live.

If this is starting to sound like a travel-guide sponsored by the Hilo Chamber of Commerce, it's only because of our never-ending enthusiasm for our favorite little city.

Hilo is home to the Hilo Campus of the University of Hawai'i and Hawai'i Junior College. The University Theater presents all sorts of incredible performances throughout the year. The newly-restored Palace Theater in the Old Downtown area also features old movies and art films as well as stage plays and cultural events. There are several fine art galleries, and all sorts of outlets for every conceivable kind of artistic endeavor.

Our little City is also home to some exceptional dining establishments, some of which feature live music most nights. And of course the hotels have regular dining extravaganzas, complete with Hawai'ian (and sometimes Tahitian) music and dance performances. Although these are intended for the tourist trade, a lot of us who live here occasionally take advantage of the fun and food, too.

For those who are dedicated shoppers, Hilo features the only genuine mall on the Island. Just about anything you could ever need is available somewhere in town, and it has been our experience that prices are not much higher than what you'd pay on the Mainland—providing you are willing to shop around. (See Chapter 6, "Shopping.")

There is a gentle, almost turn-of-the-century quality to Hilo. The Old Downtown area is being slowly restored as funds become available and is looking better every year. There are old stores that will bring back warm, nostalgic feelings to many, and right along with them are coffee houses where you can go enjoy an excellent espresso. There are mom-and-pop stores that have been in the same families for generations, and lots of new small businesses, too.

Hilo is a city of variety. It's a place where families live, work and raise their children. It really is unlike any other city or town in Hawai'i, in that the few tourists who mingle in with the residents are just people who seem to fit in, as opposed to some of the heavily touristed places where the tourist crush seems to be overwhelming at times. Nobody seems to be in a hurry in Hilo; everybody has time to be courteous and thoughtful.

The nights in Hilo are wonderful, too. The air is sweet and warm, the lights are soft and gentle, and the pace is even slower than during the day. Once each year, Hilo has it's annual Ho'olau'lea (party), where several blocks of the Old Downtown area are closed to traffic and there's just one big, gala street party! About a dozen live bands share the three music stages and play long into the night, food booths line the streets for blocks, and a few thousand happy people are walking, talking, and dancing the night away. There's even one of those old-timey giant searchlights with a beam that pierces the sky, like some theaters had back in the olden days. Are you old enough to remember those?

Hilo is the business center of this side of the Island and also the County Seat for Hawai'i County (all of the Big Island). For this reason, it's also where many of the regular jobs are found.

Hilo's "Old Town"

The residential areas of Hilo vary a lot in many ways. Most are clean and tidy, but that's where the similarity ends. Some are new developments of fancy homes in the $350,000-up category, and then there are the many older, established areas in which home sizes, styles, ages and quality vary so much that the prices go from a low of $150,000 to over $600,000. In the last year, it has become increasingly difficult to find available homes in Hilo, but they do come up. You have to be vigilant and patient. This scarcity, of course, drives up the prices, and at this point it doesn't look like they'll ever come back down. Stabilize, perhaps, but not drop. What's happening is that the Big Island is finally becoming "discovered," and the prices are beginning to catch up to the other Islands.

The size and scope of Hilo's residential areas is hard to visualize from just driving around town. You can get a better idea by taking the roads going mauka, so you can oversee the city from the hills. Also, take a look at the map of Hilo in the front of the phone book. It's an excellent street guide, too.

On your inter-Island flight from Honolulu to Hilo, get a window seat as far forward as you can and on the right side of the airplane. From this vantage point, you'll get a great view of the entire city, including the residential areas that extend up into the hills. You'll also get to view the Hamakua Coast all the way down into Hilo, and that will give you an idea of the many residential areas along the ocean.

One recent turn of events is that the University has experienced a huge increase in enrollment in the last year, and of course, this is having an effect on the availability of housing in the area. And as usual, when the supply goes down, the price goes up. While the effect is most obvious on rentals, it will carry over to home sales, as well.

Hilo has the reputation of being the rainiest city on earth. Clearly, this has not been our experience. More often than not, our weekly (and sometimes more often) trips to Hilo have found our favorite city in brilliant sunshine. We live right in Hilo now, and our "rain experience" remains intact.

University of Hawaii, Hilo Campus (A tiny portion of it!)

Our own experiences aside, it does rain a lot in Hilo and you should know that the amount of rain, like in every other place on the Island, varies a great deal with minor differences in elevation. As soon as you leave sea-level and drive up into the hills, you'll be heading into more frequent rain. The Kaumana area of Hilo is absolutely beautiful, featuring many homes with breathtaking views, but its higher elevation makes it famous for rain.

In all fairness, we have to admit that a once in a while, even after all these years, we forget the Rule of Parking: roll up your windows! (If you drive a convertible, put the top up!) Our car for years was a convertible, and sometimes we'd pull up to the grocery store on a gorgeous, sunny day, go in for some shopping, and upon our return to the car it's still sunny but the inside of the car is soaked! What happened? A squall came through. This is the kind of rain we've experienced in Hilo the most; the occasional rain-squall during a sunny day. Even though you get a little wet, it's still nice and warm and you dry right off again. Think of it as refreshing.

"All this rain" is a subjective thing, too. For example, if you're moving here from Seattle, there are two distinct differences. One thing you would notice right away is that even when it's raining, it's still warm outside. The other is that instead of a constant drizzle as you would experience in Seattle, we get our rain all at once! Hilo might get the same amount of rain as Seattle during a particular day, but Hilo gets it all in ten minutes. And then it mostly rains at night. Now on the other hand, if your last home was in Arizona, the rain might be a bit much for you. One thing you'll find here is that the folks who live here and love it don't even notice the rain. It's all part of the beauty of the Windward side. And indeed, after one of our occasional overnighters to the Kona side, we always appreciate the refreshing rain when we come back home.

The bottom line: If the thought of a home, perhaps even a gracious older home in excellent condition with a sweeping view of the city and the beautiful Hilo Bay gets you going, look around in Hilo. There are homes like that available, and although the prices are higher now than they were a year or two ago, they will never be better.

Kea'au

Moving right along, just six miles south, toward the town of Volcano on Highway 11 (mauka on the Volcano Highway), we come to Kea'au. Kea'au seems like little more than a small shopping center to folks traveling through. Matter of fact, a recent new highway project called the Kea'au Bypass means that now you can go from Hilo to the Lower Puna (Pahoa, Kapoho, Kalapana) area without even going through Kea'au any more at all.

Kea'au is a small, pleasant community of homes mostly situated on the makai side of the highway. Exploring the side roads of the area will bring you to a lot of the "private property" signs on the entries to the old mill and other lands closed to the public. One of the most beautiful beaches on this side of the Island is at the end of one of these private roads and is accessible to the public only by a long and difficult walk along the rocky coastline. Too bad about that.

Also included in the Kea'au area are many small farms and other rural properties not right within the community. Kea'au weather is not unlike Hilo, except that the slightly higher elevation makes it a little wetter and cooler.

Kea'au will also shortly be the site of a new multi-million-dollar shopping center to go along with the big new residential tracts proposed for the immediate area.

One thing Kea'au does not need is a big shopping center right outside the village. This will be the final nail in the coffin for all of the small businesses in the community. Unfortunately, the big guys who build multi-million-dollar shopping centers don't much care about the impact their projects have on the existing business community. The shops in Hilo will also suffer as a result of this project, and the increased traffic at the already busy Kea'au intersections will become the problem of those who must commute through this corridor. Too bad about that, too.

Hawai'ian Paradise Park (HPP)

On the highway from Kea'au to Pahoa (Hwy 130), this enormous residential development, also known as "HPP" or "Paradise Park," contains thousands of one-acre lots and hundreds of homes. Land and home prices are reasonable here, ranging from just over $100,000 for livable homes to well over $300,000 nice ones. The recent flood of Mainland buyers who will pay anything for that ocean view have driven the prices for ocean-front and ocean-view properties through the roof, even in this modest subdivision with dirt roads and no water or sewer lines. We've seen a number of ocean-view homes in HPP go for over $500,000. Crazy.

The ocean frontage of this development affords some fantastic views, but there is no ocean access because the whole coastline in the area is a cliff that averages around twenty feet high.

A note about the ocean-front lots in HPP, last winter we had an unusually high surf during one of the many winter storms, and believe this or not, that surf tossed boulders the size of small Toyotas up over the 20' cliff. Several of the ocean-front homeowners lost their rock walls to boulders, and a few of the rocks made it into living rooms. Quite a few homes that were not damaged by rocks got flooded by some of the huge waves that rolled right in over the cliff.

With the exception of the main roads from the highway all the way to the ocean (a distance of about four miles), all of the intersecting roads are unpaved. There are no water or sewer lines, so each home has its own water catchment and septic systems. HPP is what we like to refer to as "spotty," meaning there are beautiful homes right alongside humble ones. Same goes for the terrain. A lot of HPP looks barren and dry, while the edges of the development and the parts down near the ocean are wooded and attractive.

HPP is just 15 minutes from Hilo, so it's a desired location for many people who work in town. In Hawai'i, long commutes are unheard of and highly undesirable by most people. HPP lots and homes cost more than those in nicer areas farther out simply because of their close proximity to town. The weather in HPP is about the same as in Hilo, but it also varies within the community. As in most areas on the Island, the closer you get to the ocean, the drier the climate. The elevation climb as you go mauka brings more rain.

Orchidland

Who dreamed up these names, anyway? Were they running a "corny name contest" at the time? OK,

Orchidland, right across Highway 130 from HPP, is another large tract of lots with homes on only a small percentage of them. Again, the streets are unimproved, and in dry weather, very dusty. Homes in this development tend to be of less value than in nearby HPP. Orchidland relies on catchment water systems and individual septic systems.

Ainaloa, Hawai'ian Beaches, Hawai'ian Shores, Nanawale, and others

We'll group these together because of their similarity in many ways. They are all medium-size tracts (by East Hawai'i standards) with only part of the lots having homes on them. Nanawale is more densely populated than the other two, and the lots there are small. The prices in all are near the bottom for homes. There is a larger percentage of month-to-month rentals in these developments, and the general ambiance is not as well-kept as in other communities nearby, but has improved a lot over the last few years. For some reason, there used to be a disproportionally-high crime rate here, mostly small-time burglaries, and some domestic violence and drug-related incidents. The establishment of a very effective "neighborhood watch" a few years ago has made a dramatic change here, and although you'll still hear stories about "crime in Nanawale," it's really no longer an issue.

Most of these tracts are on catchment water systems and individual septic systems.

"Hawai'ian Shores" is the community on the right side of the main road going down into the "Hawai'ian Beaches" area and is clearly the exception to some of the above. It is a private subdivision with an Association and some rules that make for a more pleasant community. There are far fewer rentals here, and there's a private water system, eliminating the need for catchment tanks.

And in case you're wondering, there are no "shores" in Hawai'ian Shores, nor "beaches" in Hawai'ian Beaches. More creative naming at work here. As close as either community gets to shores or beaches is the cliff at the ocean's edge.

Again, weather depends on elevation. The closer to the ocean, the warmer and dryer it is.

Life in most of these communities has improved a lot in the last year or two because of their neighborhood watch programs, and a lot of support from the community. The basic philosophy of the programs is that the thieves generally cruise a neighborhood before attempting any of their mischief. If they see the occasional car with a "Neighborhood Watch Patrol" magnetic sign on the side, they know that this isn't going to be easy and they go elsewhere. It sounds to simple, perhaps, but we've seen it work in several communities now.

The really effective programs are the ones with enthusiastic community support. There will be a "phone tree," so that if somebody needs assistance or is observing something suspicious going on, there's always a neighbor close by who will respond. A potential thief who knows he is being watched is going to think twice about doing a burglary; if a neighbor shows up also sporting the "Patrol" signs on his car, the thief is out of there for good. It's all about neighbors helping neighbors.

Pahoa

About 11 miles from Kea'au and past the HPP and Orchidland subdivisions we come to Pahoa, the historic little village that time seems to have forgotten. The 100-year-old buildings and wooden sidewalks are basically unchanged over the years, although you will see newer structures here and there. In sharp contrast to the old ambiance is the new, state-of-the-art, Olympic-size swimming pool facility. Some state-wide swim meets are held here occasionally, and other than that, the pool gets little use. Perhaps it's because most of the kids here would rather play in the ocean than in a pool? It is open to the public for free daily use. The pool is located near the Community Center right in the middle of the village.

Main Street, Pahoa Town

Pahoa is the service center for a much larger geographical area than just the tiny town, as is evidenced by the huge K-12 school campus and the 1000-kid enrollment there.

You can make a day of just people-watching in Pahoa! Pahoa is reminiscent of a 60's-era small town in Northern California, with its colorful characters and old-west ambiance. There are all sorts of interesting places: excellent restaurants featuring Mexican, Chinese, Italian, vegetarian, Thai, local-style and ordinary American-style; gift and curio shops; imported clothing; two grocery stores and a brand-new natural-foods store. There's a gas station, post office, two banks, a 7-11, and an excellent hardware store and of course, a pawn shop.

There's also a brand-new small shopping center at the Hilo end of Pahoa Town now. The hardware store has moved there, and the center is being populated by the likes of Subway, another gas station, a "real" grocery store, and more! Progress comes slowly to Pahoa, but it does come.

Except for a very small area of ancient, colorful and quaint homes on the few side streets in the village, Pahoa includes very little actual residential area. There are many rural homes nearby, and the rest of the population that frequents Pahoa lives in the surrounding large tracts of homes. These include Nanawale, Leilani Estates and a few not-so-nearby: Kehena Beach Estates, Kalapana Seaview, Puna Palisades and others. These last few are all down near the end of Highway 130, about ten miles from Pahoa.

Highway 130 used to go all the way around the Island, but the lava flows of the early 90s covered enough of the road that it will probably never be rebuilt. If you like this area and would like to see some of the non-tract homes for sale, ask your Realtor to find the listings for you. We've found some very interesting places this way that we would never have come across on our own. Among them are small farms and very rural homes on small acreages upslope behind the town. The road that accesses this area goes up through the middle of the high-school campus.

Kapoho

Now we're going to take a small detour and head makai from Pahoa on Highway 132 to Kapoho. Kapoho has the reputation of being the sunniest spot on the

A Kapoho vacation-rental home with its own tidal pond

windward side of the Island, and indeed it seems to be. The three small communities in Kapoho enjoy the creatively inspired names of Beach Lots, Farm Lots and (get this!) Vacationland.

Beach Lots is the most expensive part and has some beautiful homes, fantastic ocean frontage and easy ocean access. There are calm lagoons right in some of the yards, and perfect for snorkeling or just playing in the water. Some are even heated for you by Mother Nature's geothermal springs. Homes for sale are rare, and when they come on the market they now sell for a minimum of $300,000 up to well over $1,000,000. Hardly "affordable." With some notable exceptions, most of the homes are on small lots, as is the case with most ocean-front property. The bigger parcels of land are very pricey. But don't despair; if you really take a liking to Beach Lots, you can still occasionally find small, older homes needing upgrading in this gated oceanfront community for a manageable price. When it happens, it doesn't take long for the house to sell, so you have to stay on top of the market here. The whole Kapoho area has been, as they say, discovered, and much of it is being bought up by folks who use their purchases as vacation rentals until the time that they can retire there.

The Farm Lots area is comprised of five-acre lots zoned as farm land, or in zoning-speak, "AG" for agriculture. Many of these have been bought for that purpose and most of those are orchid farms with the owners' homes on the property. Some get bought by folks with no farming intentions but who just want more privacy. The lots are currently going for $100,000 and up. The terrain varies from flat to sloping, and the vegetation is heavy on some lots and sparse on others. Since there are already quite a few established flower farms in this area, you need to know that there is chemical spraying going on. If you get interested in a place in the Farm Lots, it's a good idea to make sure it is upwind from any flower farms or possible future flower farms. The reason is that if you are downwind, you'll be in the wind path of all the spraying. Basically, this means finding a lot on the ocean side of the subdivision.

Last but not least, we come to Vacationland, a curious little community of homes ranging from big and expensive to tiny but not cheap. A few years ago, it was hard to give away a home here. Now it's hard to keep one on the market for more than a few weeks. Two years ago, a two-bedroom house on one of the 8,000 square-foot lots would go for as little as $100,000, and a big, two-story home with a fantastic tidal pond in the back yard sold for $285,000. Tiny ocean-front cabins were been bringing the then-unbelievable prices of $140,000 and up, but the homes a few blocks from the beach were still reasonable.

That was then. Now, the little houses back where there is no ocean view sell for $250,000 and up. A tiny shack on stilts right on the ocean recently went for over half a million dollars. These prices are nothing short of insane, and it is the Mainland buyer delirium that is driving it. The current low interest rates combined with the frenzied attitude of buyers who come here for a week determined to leave as property owners—at any cost—are creating an unreal market for ocean-front properties.

Vacationland has had a reputation as a kind of rough place, and to a degree it still is. There is a notorious group of about six homes right in the center of the community, all owned by the same person and all rented to folks who don't seem to have a lot of pride in their environs. The evidence is the obvious lack of maintenance of homes and yards and in some cases, the colorful bed-sheets used as curtains. But it's easy to avoid this little area and the rest of the community is nice. Not fancy or the least bit upscale, but nice.

The upside is that these homes (there were eight when the last edition of this book went to press) are being bought by people who care about the community and they are being totally refurbished and brought back to life. If there is a positive side to all this new interest in East Hawai'i real estate, it is this slow-but-sure conversion of some of the worst areas into some of the nicest.

There are new homes being built in Vacationland, and our feeling is that it won't be long before the whole community is thoroughly cleaned up. Building new seems to be the best way to go right now, because the lot prices are still comparably low. Nice ones *not* on the ocean are selling for $50-100,000.

The location of this little community is awesome, and has a fantastic ocean access with calm, tide pools and reef-protected swimming and snorkeling. The marine-life and coral formations are unique to this area and bring lots of weekend visitors, making the ocean access area crowded on those days. There is talk in the community of installing a gate like at Beach Lots to keep the vehicle traffic down to those who live there. All three of these Kapoho communities have County water available, but not all the homes are hooked up. New hookups run from $6,000 and up, when available, and they're not always available. For this reason, many homes are still on catchment systems, and all are on private septic systems.

These ocean-front communities have transcended any possible definition of "affordable," and probably the only reason we're even bothering to talk this much about them is to illustrate what is going on here now.

Leilani Estates

Here is where you'll find one of the best values in homes! The catch, and we'll expose it right up front, is most of Leilani is too rainy for a lot of people. That said, Leilani is one of the most beautiful, well-kept and safest communities on the Island. It consists of about 2,000 one-acre lots, most of them over 400 feet deep. The depth of the lots prompts most residents to build far back on their property, giving the community a unique look. Many of the homes cannot be seen from the roads. All you see is an inviting curvy driveway heading back through lush, green forest and dazzling flowers. There are some pretty basic homes in Leilani, and there are some very special ones as well. In only the very top few streets of Leilani Estates, the roads are unpaved and this small area is not covered by Leilani's Owners Association minimal rules or restrictions. In this small area of Leilani, you can sometimes find homes at unbelievable prices. Some of them will be funky, owner-built places, but if you're on a serious budget, check it out!

Prices for decent homes in the main subdivision range from around $120,000 to over $500,000. There are a few lots that offer an ocean view, and homes on those lots will be higher yet. Lots, which only five years ago went for $6000, now bring from $20,000 to $50,000 for all but the few (distant) ocean-view parcels, and they bring $100,000 and up.

There are still a huge number of vacant lots in Leilani, so it seems hard to justify the price increase in lots. Some diligent research might come up with some pleasant surprises.

Strange as it might seem to folks who commute for an hour each way, every day, the cost of homes in Leilani is kept down by the 35 minute drive to Hilo. Folks here just don't do mainland-style commutes.

When we lived in Leilani, I would occasionally advertise a car for sale in the paper. Somebody would call from Hilo and when he found out I lived in Leilani he'd get mad at me. "I don't drive that far to take my family on vacation," he'd tell me and then hang up. The way we look at it is the drive to Hilo (or anywhere else on the Island, for that matter) is so beautiful and the traffic is never a problem, so why not just enjoy it?

Back to the rain part, Leilani varies about 400 feet in elevation from the upper portion to the lower end, and the upper part, at about 1000 feet in elevation, is the rainiest. It's obvious when you drive through, that the upper part, nearest the highway, is a lush, dense rain forest, and as the name implies, it takes a lot of moisture to keep it green. The forest becomes more sparse as the elevation drops, and just that little change in elevation is enough to make a significant difference in the rainfall.

When we lived there, we were closer to the bottom than to the top, and sometimes we'd be on the phone with a friend who lived nearer the top and he'd talk of how hard it was raining while it was sunny at our house. The cooler elevation of Leilani is preferred by some folks because the temps usually run about 10 degrees less on any given day than at sea level. The rule-of-thumb is that the temp drops about ten degrees per thousand feet elevation. Of course there are exceptions, but that's why it's called a rule-of-thumb!

Leilani has had a very effective "neighborhood watch" program going on for some years now, and because of it, it's one of the safest subdivisions on the Island. During our seven years there, we seldom locked anything. We left the keys in our cars and the house was nearly always open.

Leilani is also a very well maintained community. The roadsides are kept neatly mowed, which is a major job, what with the many miles of road and the rate of growth of everything! The pavement is kept in good repair and the whole subdivision has a nice feel to it when driving through. The deep lots mean that there will almost never be a car parked on the street, which in itself gives a different kind of feeling.

A house-hunting tip for anywhere on the Island: Take note of the vegetation around you. If you're in a lush rain forest, even if it happens to be a sunny and bright day, please believe that it rains a lot there. That's why it's a rain forest. We've heard from a few folks who bought in Leilani during some great, sunny weather only to be disappointed later when they saw how much it rained there. Again, a lot of rain to one person is just the right amount to another. Some folks would rather it never rained and others couldn't live without it. Best you feel it for yourself. One other thing to watch for in Leilani, as in any other place here that gets a lot of rain is evidence of mildew. Mildew can be a real problem in some places, and it's usually evident as black, sooty-looking deposits on exterior walls, rafters and any other places outside that don't get a lot of air flow or sunlight. Inside, mildew is often first noticed by its smell. The odor bothers some folks a lot and others not at all. Interior mildew can be found in dark places like closets and even on walls behind doors that are seldom closed. Don't forget to look up, too, as mildew likes to accumulate on ceilings in rooms with little air flow or sunlight.

Kalapana and Vicinity

From Pahoa, we head down Highway 130 (called the Pahoa-Kalapana Highway) to Kalapana. Kalapana was once the site of the famous Kalapana Black Sand Beach, which sadly got covered with a thick, wide layer of lava in the early '90s. There are rural homes (homes not in communities and possibly on larger lots than are normally found in tracts) and even some small communities off of this highway between Pahoa and Kalapana, and if you're into seclusion, you can find some bargains here. Whenever you see a home listed for sale for way under $100,000, it's likely you'll find it in this area. Some of these small subdivisions are run-down, have substandard owner-built houses and reputations that are less than inviting, so be careful and look closely. As you peruse the offerings, let your intuition be your guide.

Kehena Beach Estates

Where Highway 130 dead-ends into Highway 137 (the Red Road), we'll take a left. Now we're driving through some dry, scrubby terrain, and in a couple of miles we come to a sudden change of scenery: a lush tropical forest! Just into the forest is the little community of Kehena Beach Estates, or more commonly, just Kehena. This is an area of small lots with homes that range from tiny to huge, from humble to finely-crafted, and in prices from $150,000 to over $300,000 for homes with no ocean view. Ocean-view homes and those right on the ocean bring $500,000 and up. Prices in this community have doubled in the last two years.

Some of the pricey offerings are on more than one lot, which creates better options for building, as the lots are so small. It's a friendly community of folks from all walks of life, some young, some old, mostly self-employed or not working straight jobs for one reason or another.

One of the big attractions of living here is the actual Kehena Beach, a gorgeous little black sand beach only a short walk from anywhere in the community. The beach itself is down a short-but-steep trail, and when you get down there you're in another world. The beach is small, only about 300 feet long. It's a crescent of shimmering black sand nestled into a 30-foot-high cliff, with palms and all sorts of tropical growth adding to the primeval ambiance. This is a clothing-optional beach, but it's also very much a family place, where on any given day you'll see kids from 2 to 82 playing in the surf, enjoying the warm sun, and in a climate of peace and quiet. Some people are clothed, others are not, and nobody seems to care. Often there will be somebody gently strumming a guitar or maybe even the strains of a flute coming from somewhere in the distance.

On many mornings, you can watch pods of spinner dolphins frolicking close enough to the shore that people will swim out to play with them. It really is a special place.

Kehena recently had electric lines run in but a number of homes are still on solar systems. The community relies on catchment water and individual septic systems. The weather here is usually clear and sunny, even when it's raining elsewhere close by. Kehena is a special place for special people. It's not one of those middle-of-the-road communities; you'll either love it or it won't do a thing for you.

The caveats about Kehena are mosquitoes and people of ill repute. The dense rain-forest ambiance that makes Kehena so special on one level is also what attracts the mosquitoes, and they are a real problem there. The other issue is that for some reason, perhaps it is the beach and the people it attracts, Kehena gets more than its share of petty burglaries and car break-ins in the parking areas by the beach. If this area feels good to you, get to know some of the residents there and talk to them.

Kalapana Seaview and Puna Palisades

Both of these tracts are walking distance to Kehena Beach (see above description) and both have ocean-view parcels and homes. Both are sparsely populated at this point, but there is definite building activity going on. Palisades (another of those inspired names) feels much better to us, in that it's smaller and the homes are of a more consistent quality. Among nicer homes, Seaview has some that you have to wonder how they withstand a good breeze without collapsing. Both communities have electric power but no water or sewers.

Catchment systems are the norm for domestic water. The power came in recently, so there are still homes there on solar systems, and most of them are substandard at best. Beware when looking at a home that the owner says is "on solar." If you have no experience with this sort of thing but are open to looking into it, be sure to have the home checked out by a solar contractor before you get real serious. Probably all you need do is take a list of the major components to any solar contractor to find out if the system can be expected to support the house. Most cannot, and the owners run noisy little generators to supplement their power needs.

Prices in Palisades are higher than Seaview, but even so, when homes come on the market there, fairly decent ones go for around $200,000 and up. Again, sunshine is the order of the day here. Both communities are barren when compared to Kehena, and most of the tree-cover and landscaping you'll see there has been done by the residents. Some folks prefer the sparse vegetation to being in a dense forest, and in the Kehena-to-Seaview area you certainly have your choice.

Although this may be just our opinion, we feel that Palisades is a bit more, well, let's say civilized than Seaview. There are some residents of Seaview who have been there for many years and they resent what some folks think of as progress. They would prefer to keep things as they have always been and they feel that the newcomers are expecting to clean up the community to the detriment of the old-timers. There is a community association of sorts, and we've heard some very colorful stories about the rather bizarre goings-on at their meetings.

Be careful here, and do your homework!

Kurtistown, Mountain View, Glenwood

Kurtistown, Mountain View and Glenwood are all communities on Highway 11, the Volcano Highway. They are all situated along the Highway starting just mauka of Kea'au. Surrounding the residential areas are the small farms that supply most of the produce that you'll find in our farmers' markets and some of what you'll find in the stores. (Curiously, most of the produce in Hawai'i's stores is imported from the Mainland.) The elevation of this area is just high enough that it rains a lot. It's one of those places that on a nice, sunny day, it looks irresistibly green and lush, but careful inspection reveals there are no sprinklers anywhere to keep it that way. If your passion is growing things, especially edibles, you couldn't find a more prolific place. If you aspire to having a small organic farm, look no farther. Home prices are quite reasonable, but since the size and quality of the homes and the land they are on vary so much it's difficult to quote actual numbers. This is one of those places you'll need to feel for yourself.

There are places deep in forest, others on rolling hills with spectacular views, and still others in small tracts of homes. Lot sizes vary from tiny to huge acreages.

There are also several large residential subdivisions in this area, and home prices are substantially lower than in Hilo. Many of the homes are fairly new Mainland-style tract houses in nicely-maintained neighborhoods, so if that's your desire, check it out.

Volcano Village

Volcano Village is reminiscent of many cozy, wooded areas of the Pacific Northwest. It's usually cool and foggy or rainy, also like those parts of the Pacific Northwest. There are attractive, narrow, curvy roads with lovely homes nestled into the woods, and you'll even catch the aroma of wood-burning stoves as you explore here. The ambiance of Volcano Village is not the first thing that comes to mind when one thinks of Hawai'i, but for many it is the real Paradise. You'll find some popular vacation-rentals and B&Bs in this area, and one of the finest restaurants on the Island is in the village.

Homes are moderate in price, ranging from a low of just over $100,000 to as much as you'd like to pay. Compared to the same size home available in many of the Puna subdivisions, Volcano is expensive. Compared to Hilo prices, it is reasonable.

For some reason, the prices in this area have not escalated in step with some of the other regions, but this might be temporary. If it turns out that you feel really good here, now is the time!

Volcano Village is considered by most of the folks who live there as a pretty exclusive area. At about 26 miles from Hilo, it isn't a very long drive, and the highway is excellent and rarely congested. This is another place you have to really feel for yourself, because it is so very different from any other place on the Island. You have to like cool and rainy weather year 'round, and even be able to deal with some occasional frost in the winter.

On the opposite side of the highway from the Village is Mauna Loa Estates, a development of lots and homes that is more reminiscent of the Lower Puna developments. The streets are mostly straight and at right angles to each other, the homes are sparsely scattered throughout the tract of lots, and most of the homes are less expensive than those in the Village. There are some distinct exceptions, though, as people are building some really fine homes there now. So if you like that cooler climate but would rather not be in the dense forest, this might be what you're looking for. The area is forested, but the forest is younger than in the village, so the trees are all smaller. A lot of the area is more brushy than forested, too.

Vog alert! This the first opportunity we've had to introduce you to vog. Vog is volcanic haze, air-pollution that comes from our active volcano. Some of it comes directly from the volcano's vent, but most is from the reaction of hot lava running into the ocean. Vog is a real problem on the Kona side of the Island, as the normal tradewinds carry it off to the west and then around that side. Except for the few days a year when we experience a "Kona wind," a wind coming from the Kona side, we seldom get vog on the Windward side. If there is an exception to this, it would be Volcano. For some reason, the topography in the area seems to invite a certain amount of vog over the hills into the Volcano area from time to time, so this needs to be considered. Mostly, the negative effect of vog is how it obscures our famous sunsets (and the view in general), but it also has its health hazards. People with any kinds of respiratory problems should avoid vog exposure.

News Flash: As I sit here in our ocean-view living room on this warm and sunny January day, it pains me to report that there is, in fact, no ocean view at all today. We are experiencing the worst case of vog here in Hilo that we've ever had, and it has been going on for some two weeks now. Supposedly, it is because of a persistent dry Kona Wind. It is really sad to look out toward the ocean and have it look like Kona. There's a thick, gray-brown haze out there that completely obscures everything farther away than about one mile. According to our somewhat unreliable weather gurus, we will get some relief in another few days.

Wood Valley

Wood Valley is a mystical, magical, peaceful and quiet place. It's a small rural community nestled into a valley that affords some awesome views.

There aren't often many homes or even lots for sale in this area, and when they come on the market they are usually fairly pricey compared to other rural properties. The prices vary widely depending on the size, location and useful area of the parcel. The whole area is hilly so there isn't a lot of level land.

Although this whole region is fairly dry, Wood Valley does enjoy some afternoon and evening rains.

Wood Valley is home to the Wood Valley Buddhist Temple and Retreat Center, an unbelievably beautiful and tranquil place nestled into a verdant hillside. There is a year 'round schedule of all kinds of spiritual and healing-arts retreats and workshops.

The long distance to supplies and jobs has kept Wood Valley sparsely populated and the real estate prices lower than what might be expected in such a beautiful area.

Wood Valley can get vog from time to time if the wind is just right. Most of the time, the only vog you'll experience is what you can see of it in the view toward the ocean, but occasionally, it does drift up into the valley.

The nearest town to Wood Valley is Pahala, on Highway 11 and about ten minutes makai. Driving time to Hilo is about an hour, so this would not be a good place to live for anyone needing to make frequent trips.

Pahala

Here are some real housing bargains! Pahala, situated about halfway between Volcano and Na'alehu, is a sleepy little town of mostly older homes. It has a quaint charm and is neat and tidy, even though many of the homes show their ages. This is another of the many casualties of the sugar industry, and unlike some towns that have picked themselves up and developed a new source of income and commerce, for this town, time seems to be standing still. The way things are going here, it won't be too long before this turns around, because the bargains are just too good.

Again, even here things are changing. Only a couple years ago, older homes in very restorable condition would go for give-away prices, like well under $100,000. Rents here were also cheap, often under $500 a month for a decent 3-bedroom home. Of course, with the hour's drive to Hilo, Pahala is best suited to those who won't need to make the trip often.

Homes in Pahala are not often on the market, and now when they are, the prices are higher than even a year ago, but still a lot less than a comparable home in or near Hilo.

It's hot and dry here most of the time, so this is a place for sun lovers!
A 10-minute drive will take you to Punalu'u Black Sand Beach, which is a great place for swimming and playing in the surf. The proximity to the beach, Volcanoes National Park and a golf course make it seem like some day this, too, will become developed as a tourist destination. Want to start a B&B?

Na'alehu and Vicinity

Na'alehu, in the so-far undeveloped Ka'u District, is a picturesque, friendly little village that is about as typically "local style" as you'll find anywhere on the Island. The part of town you'll see while driving through is just a few blocks of small businesses, a few homes right on the highway, a church and a big park on the makai side of the road. There are also homes and farms tucked away in the areas around the village.

Na'alehu is a long way from supplies, entertainment and just about everything else, so you have to really like being out in the country to make your home here. The drive to either Hilo or Kailua is well over an hour, and these are the only sources for major supplies, hardware and other staples of day-to-day living.

In recent months, we have seen numerous mentions in our local papers about development planned for this pristine area. The local folks are extremely concerned about the possibility (probability?) of the residential development that is being proposed. Actually, it's happening already, with large agricultural lots being subdivided and aggressively marketed. One realtor sent our a blanket mailing of flyers that announced, "We will sell you the heart and soul of Ka'u." Not good.

Ka'u District weather is usually dry and warm. Curiously, when it does rain here, it really rains and there have been some dramatic flood situations in the last few years. Because there are so few homes in this area, properties for sale in the Na'alehu area are few and far between. When they do come up, prices reflect the long distance from the Island's two major business districts.

H.O.V.E.

Hawai'ian Ocean View Estates, most often simply called Ocean View or HOVE, is a huge tract of lots, mostly on an old lava flow with spotty vegetation. Barren is a word that comes to mind. Properties here are among the least expensive on the Island, and among the reasons for this are the long drive to Kailua-Kona, the topography, and the air-quality. Often, vog hangs in the air here so that the ocean, only a short distance away, is barely visible through the haze. People with respiratory problems need to be especially aware of the locations of vog areas when trying to assess a future home site. It is possible to be in one of these places on one of the few days when there is very light vog (or even none), and jump into buying a property only to find out later about the vog.
Immediately adjacent to HOVE, on the mauka side of the highway, are two smaller subdivisions: Kona Kai View

Estates and Hawai'ian Ranchos. The weather for this whole area is best described as hot and dry.

Some of the least expensive properties on the Island can be found in the HOVE area, and when you're looking in "Homes and Land" and see what seems like a real bargain on a property that appears to be on the Kona side, it will probably be in HOVE.

The whole portion of the Island from HOVE to Kailua gets heavily impacted with vog a lot of the time, but there have been several short spells when the volcano stopped pumping lava into the ocean and the sky was brilliant and clear. As lovely as West Hawai'i is during one of these rare times, this is not a good time to be looking for real estate!

The vog thing seems to bother some people a lot more than it does others. We've talked to tourists and friends who had just experienced the Kona side for the first time and some say they didn't even notice it, while others complain about sore throats and no more "famous Kona sunsets." Many of the people who live there year 'round say, "What vog?" Even so, not being able to see the ocean horizon trough the haze, and then the occasional bad-day vog warnings on the radio make it hard to ignore that vog is a reality for many. You just have to experience it for yourself to see if might be a problem for you.

On Toward Kailua Town

The South Kona area is blossoming with new homes in many tiny subdivisions, most of them being up near the highway. Some are just mauka of the highway and others reach from the highway as far downslope as the terrain will accommodate. Several are so steep that traversing the main roads is right on the edge of scary. There are even a few small beaches along this route, but they are mostly at the ends of long, steep, twisty roads. The home prices here are attractive and if you like the environs, this is a good place for bargain hunting.

Dogs, Again

Dogs? What happened to our tour? Well, I know, this is totally off the subject, but right now it is about 6:30 on a quiet, beautiful evening. I'm here in our living room with my trusty laptop, and although we are blessed to be living in a relatively dog-free neighborhood, there is a yappy little dog going off that has been continuously yap-yap-yapping for about an hour now. Non-stop. Yap-yap-yap. I'm just bringing it up because of how pervasive the dog-noise thing is here and how important it is to be mindful of it when you go house hunting. This is just one little dog, and it only does this occasionally, but when it goes off, apparently its owners don't care, don't notice, or maybe they are amused by the noise. It goes on for long periods, sometimes several hours at a time. In any event, it is driving me nuts! Sorry.

Moving Right Along . . .

Honaunau, Captain Cook, Kealakekua and Holualoa

We're now well up on the Kona side of the Island. We'll group these areas together because they are all in the same general area. Honaunau is a residential area between the highway and the ocean and has many inviting, twisty streets with homes ranging from humble to extravagant. Homes here now start at around $200,000 for a modest fixer, and the sky is the limit on the high end of prices. It's mostly hilly with little level land available, but with good tree cover in most places. Many of the homes here, even the humble ones, feature beautiful tropical landscaping.

Captain Cook and Kealakekua are centered on the highway that runs upslope from the ocean through this whole area. Ocean views from up here are "distant" views, but some are spectacular anyway. The cooler temperatures at this elevation make the area desirable for those who don't deal well with the often over 90 degree temps closer to sea-level. This whole stretch of highway is a commercial zone, so residents can find shopping, restaurants and even hardware, furniture and appliances. There are many coffee farms around here, and some are usually on the market at any given time. Most of them are small operations of a few acres with a home.

Again, the caveat here is the vog. When the Kona side gets a dose of vog, this is the area that gets it the worst. On the bad days, it is difficult to see the ocean at all from here. It would be a good idea to spend some time if you become interested in possible residence in this area. In all fairness, some folks who live in the vog areas claim to not notice it. Like, what vog? They also claim they have never heard of anyone complaining about associated health issues. Type "vog-Hawai'i" into a search utility for more info.

This whole region is the one remaining place where you will still find a lot of leasehold properties for sale. Especially up in "coffee country," which covers most of the properties on both sides of the highway, there are many small acreages with homes and coffee farms. When you see a listing for a three acre producing coffee farm with a nice home, all for an unbelievable price, it's most likely a leasehold property. We cover the caveats of leasehold properties elsewhere, but please check out any leasehold offerings very carefully! Depending on your personal situation, a leasehold property could work well for you but again, many of the leases are near their renegotiation times and the new "adjusted" rates can be real deal-breakers.

Just a little farther up the road and immediately mauka of Kailua Village is the small, picturesque community of Holualoa. Known as an artist's community, this area is hilly and again, has little level land. The main street (the highway that runs through all of the preceding communities) has a number of galleries, all featuring the excellent works of local-area artists. There is also a fine coffee shop renown for mouth-watering pastries, fruit smoothies and well-prepared espresso drinks. Homes here are not often on the market and when they do become available they are usually upward of $300,000. Occasionally, though, smaller or fixer-upper places come on the market for about half that amount. This is one of those places where it's good to talk to the local folks if you're serious about finding a home. As you visit the galleries and the coffee shop, ask questions about any properties for sale. You might just be pleasantly surprised!

Kailua-Kona

Kailua-Kona, Kailua Village, Kailua and Kona are all names that you will hear used to describe the same area. The reason for the confusion is that Kona is actually a *District* (much like a county on the Mainland) and the tourist destination of Kailua Village just happens to be in that district. So for some, it's "We're going to Kona this year for our vacation." The actual name of the Village is Kailua, but since there is also a "Kailua" on several of the other Islands, that's a source of confusion in itself. "Kailua-Kona" is an accurate way of describing the town of Kailua, as it shows the name of the town ahead of the

Ali'i Drive, Kailua Kona

name of the District it's in. In the interests of clarity, we have chosen "Kailua Village" to describe the immediate village area that includes all the hotels, restaurants, condos and tourist facilities. Within the Village, we also include all of the residential subdivisions listed below. "Kailua-Kona," includes all of the above plus the subdivisions both industrial areas that are toward the airport from the Village. Whew!

To live in Kailua-Kona, you would have to enjoy the faster-moving tourist energy that is pervasive there. We enjoy being there for an occasional day or two, but then when we get all wound up in that energy it feels so good to come back home to the peace and tranquility of the Hilo side. For sure, there are those who love this kind of ambiance, and perhaps Kailua-Kona is their paradise. If you are one of these people, there are usually a few affordable homes available in and around the Village.

If you like the hotter, drier climate near the ocean, there are also homes within a few blocks from the water that fall into the affordable category. They'll be either small or in need of repairs, or both. We've seen some great offerings on multi-family places in this area, too, which could offer a home with a built-in income. Upslope, the vicinities of Captain Cook and Kealakekua offer cooler temperatures and less noise and traffic. It also often rains here in the late afternoons and evenings, further keeping things greener and cooler.

Keep in mind that the prices of nearly everything you'll ever need are higher here than when you get out of tourist-land. To some that could add up to a significant amount after a while, particularly if you need to drive a lot and have to buy gasoline at tourist prices. If you are skilled in frugal living, though, you can still manage it here once you find an affordable home.

The residential subdivisions close in to Kailua Village are where you will find the best home buys. We've included most of them here so that you'll know where they are if you see homes advertised. Some are very upscale, but they'll be easy to identify when you look at the listed home prices. After a while, you'll get to recognize the subdivision names that always have the lowest prices. As in most subdivisions, the lots tend to be small and the homes fairly close together. Because of the hilly terrain immediately mauka of the Village, many of even the lowest priced homes have great ocean views. Here's a list of the subdivisions close in to Kailua Village:

Kailua Estates
Kona Heights
Kuakini Makai
Kamani Trees
Kilohana Kai
Kailua View Estates
Kona Vistas
Kona Orchards
Ilolani
Lono Kona
Aloha Kona
Alii Kai
White Sands Estates
Kahalu'u Beachlots
Kahalu'u Bay Villas

The residential subdivisions on the airport side of the Village are—with a few exceptions—less expensive than the ones we just explored. Most are accessed from the highway going from the Village up to Kamuela (Waimea), Highway 190, also known as Mamalahoa Highway. Most are on steep hillsides, making possible some expansive views but no level land. Note that the views here are "expansive" rather than "great." Of course, that's a personal opinion, but from up in these hills, the view is mostly barren lava flows, a view of the airport and on those days when you can see it through the distant haze, the ocean.

When looking at homes in these areas, pay attention to any difficulty you (or the real estate salesperson) might be having getting in and out of driveways. Some of the roads are actually steep enough to make this a concern. Visualize yourself living there and dealing with the lack of level land around your home. To some this is not an issue, but to others it can be a big deal after a while, especially to those who enjoy puttering around in the garden. The names of these subdivisions are as follows:

Kona Acres
Kona Heavens
Pu'uhonua Estates
Kona Wonderview
Kona Highlands
Keahole Heights
Makaula
Coastview
Palisades
Kaloko Houselots

Kaloko Heights
Kona Panoi
Kona Hills Estates
Kealakehe Estates
Kona Macadamia Acres
Harbor View
Queen Liliuokalani Village
Hale Palani
Kailua Heights
Jacaranda Gardens
Paniolo Country
Kawaihae

Kawaihae

Kawaihae seems to be extraordinarily ripe for development. It consists of an industrial area that contains shipping docks and fuel-storage facilities, a small boat harbor, a tiny shopping complex, several excellent restaurants and a small housing tract just upslope from the highway. There is an area on the Kona side of Kawaihae being developed for another housing tract, and this is no doubt just the beginning. Kawaihae, the location for the infamous movie, "Waterworld," is in the middle of some of the most spectacular ocean anywhere on the Island. The classic picture-postcard Hapuna Beach State Park is only a five-minute drive toward Kona, as are many other perfect beaches.

These areas, plus the ever-sunny weather, are the big attractions here, and it seems that the availability of fresh water is about all that has kept Kawaihae from becoming another busy resort town. For those who would like to live in or near Kawaihae in the near future, the only option is one of the homes (mostly duplexes) in the little community. These are seldom for sale, and when they do come on the market, they run $200,000 and up.

Weather here: hot and dry. If daily sunshine and easy access to world-class beaches are important to you, find a way to live here!

As in each of the places we visit on our tour, earning your living is always a consideration. If you will be among those who need to find a job, this is probably not a good place to live. If you're ready to "bring your job with you," this might indeed be your special place. See Chapter 7, "Income Opportunities."

Hawi and Kapa'au

There is no residential development anywhere north of Kawaihae until you get to the northern tip of the Island. (Well, there is one, but it's so expensive we'll just go right on by.) At the northern end, you'll find the lovely communities of Hawi and Kapa'au. They are close enough together that they seem almost as one. Both were sugar-mill communities, and when the mills closed down, these two enterprising spots fast became artist's communities of some repute. There are many galleries here, and one of the best restaurants on the Island, The Bamboo Restaurant, is a "must-do" when you visit here. Also featured inside the restaurant is another fine gallery of arts, crafts and woodworking.

Residential areas here are sparse, and are found mostly close to the two villages, on both sides of the highway, plus a few subdivisions upslope. The affordable homes in

and around Hawi and Kapa'au are limited to what the
Realtors there like to call "cute starter homes." That's
Realtor-speak for tiny and probably in need of some
serious TLC. These homes, which are mostly old

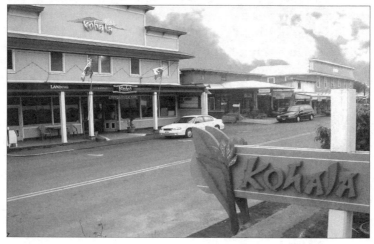

Main Street in Hawi

plantation homes with two tiny bedrooms and one tiny
bath start at around $200,000, so you would have to have a
real passion for the area to make it worthwhile. It's
another of those places you just have to feel for yourself.
One good way to find leads on homes for sale is to ask
around. Ask in the galleries and other little shops. Often
these folks know of people who are thinking of selling and
haven't yet contacted a Realtor. It's worth a try.

     Be aware that it rains a lot here and that you need
to be wary of high-wind areas, too. Look at the trees
around you, and if they're all permanently bent in the same
direction, you'll know there's a strong, prevailing wind
there even if the day you visit happens to be calm and

serene. The windy spots can be very locally specific (and very windy), and the trees do tell the tale.

From Kapa'au, we'll head up to Waimea. The highway that encircles the Island comes to an abrupt halt a few miles past Kapa'au because from that point on down to the Waipio Valley the terrain is totally road-proof.

Waimea (Kamuela)

There's a story about how come Waimea is also called Kamuela. It seems that back in the early Parker Ranch days when Waimea consisted of a post office and the few stores that supported the ranch population, the postmaster was a gentleman named Kamuela. So when there were letters or packages anywhere else on the Island

Mauna Kea from Kamuela (Yes, that's snow!)

that were headed for Waimea, the carriers were told to "take this up to Kamuela." After enough years of this, Waimea got to be called Kamuela to the point where the name stuck, which actually relieved a certain amount of confusion since most of the Islands have a town called Waimea.

Here we have a unique higher-elevation (read: cold) village that features two distinct climates. They are known as "Dry Side" and "Wet Side." The Wet Side is the Windward (or Hilo) side, and the weather there is mostly cool, moist and often foggy. The Dry Side transition happens about where the highway from Hawi and Kawaihae (Highway 19) intersects Highway 190, the one going from Hilo to Kailua-Kona.

It really is quite amazing to be driving from the Hilo side, up through this lush, green and rainy forest, then into Kamuela Town (we prefer Kamuela to Waimea) and then as you pass through the little community all of a sudden all you see is miles of dusty-dry range grass and prickly-pear cactus!

Both sides of Kamuela have nice, tidy residential areas. There are occasionally (very modest) homes available in the $175,000 range and then up—way up. There are several small subdivisions on the Wet Side that feature all sizes and styles of homes from tiny cabins to big and lavish estates. In these areas is where you'll find the lowest-cost housing.

The weather on the Wet Side can be warm and pleasant during the summer-month days, but is more often than not cool and wet. A fog lives nearly constantly in the surrounding hills and it flows gently down into these small, forested communities. There are a lot of folks who would live nowhere else, and they enjoy the cool climate and their wood stoves.

On the Dry Side, it seldom rains and it is warmer during the days. The evenings do cool off and are usually 10-20 degrees cooler than at sea level. Summers can bring

78-80-degree days and 50-60-degree nights, but we've experienced 40-degree nights at any time of the year when coming home from the Kona side. We always make sure we have enough gas to get us over the mountain so we won't have to get out of the car in Kamuela! Frosts are not uncommon on winter nights, and those who live in Kamuela keep a supply of warm clothes and a pile of firewood ready year 'round. The normal attire in Kamuela is quite similar to what you would see in Oregon or maybe Seattle; an interesting observation for us folks who live at sea level and are used to shorts and rubber slippers.

If you do your shopping in Kamuela, be prepared to pay more for everything. Gasoline is generally the highest price on the Island, usually about 20 cents higher than Hilo and even higher than in touristy Kailua-Kona. Groceries and even the farmer's market offerings are higher as well.

Honoka'a

A 15-minute downhill drive through some exquisite countryside takes you to the neat little town of Honoka'a. Often, a few minutes before arriving in Honoka'a, you will find yourself driving out from under Kamuela's cloud cover and into bright. clear sunshine. Another would-be casualty of the sugar industry, this little town picked itself up and turned itself into a tourist attraction and an active and desirable location for living in general. The main street is lined with new and old businesses, including several good restaurants, coffee shops, antique stores, galleries and much more. A star attraction is the Honoka'a People's Theater, a beautifully and lovingly restored old theater that now features many musical and cultural events. The annual week-long music festival brings in musicians from around the world and nearly every night is a sell-out. The old-time flavor of the community has been well preserved while cleaning up the store fronts.

The road to Waipio Valley goes through the town, and the residential areas are scattered all the way from the main highway (Highway 19) to Waipio. Homes are rarely available for under $200,000 here, and most are substantially higher. This is one of the places that if it feels right to you, you would do well to spend some time there and drive every street looking for "for sale" signs. The Realtors, while they do a good job finding listings, don't get them all. Some sellers prefer to not go through a Realtor, and some of these folks and their offerings can actually be found by asking storekeepers, waitresses and others if they happen to know of any homes for sale. You never know until you try! If you find a for-sale-by-owner (FSBO) property and you would prefer to avail yourself of the services of a Realtor, you can still do that, too. The catch is that you (not the seller) will be paying the Realtor's commission, although that commission can generally be negotiated down from the prevailing six percent.

Laupahoehoe

We skipped right over some residential areas between Honoka'a and here because they are best found by actually exploring every side road that looks interesting. With a few exceptions, most of them are tiny plantation villages with old, small homes very close together. The exceptions are a few small tracts of newer homes and some small acreages.

Another exception, and this is a new (two years) phenomenon, are the many new small subdivisions of what was once sugar-cane land. There are many such subdivisions between Honoka'a and Hilo now, and most are divided up into 20-acre (and bigger) lots. When this rampant subdividing began about two years ago, these lots sold for around $200,000 and up. Now it's hard to find any for less than twice that amount. As with the rest of the real estate picture here, it has gone nuts. There is no shortage of cash buyers for these properties, and they sell as soon as they are put on the market.

Kolopa, just a few miles toward Hilo from Honoka'a is all mauka of the highway and goes way up into the cooler elevations. There are homes and small farms scattered along this road from the highway all the way to the top. Again, take a drive up the road if you lean toward the cooler elevations and see what it feels like to you. For folks who like the cooler climes, there are some beautiful settings all through this peaceful and quiet area, some with incredible far-reaching views, too.

There is a small and lovely residential area in Laupahoehoe, and we listed it because of its road right down to the ocean. With the exception of a couple of surf spots near Hilo where rivers run to the ocean, this is one of the only ocean access points along the highway from Honoka'a to Hilo. You can find some homes along the road to the ocean, but be forewarned that this is a very steep road with nearly no level land along its way, and because it is an East-facing cliff, the sun sets early in the afternoon there. The residential portion of Laupahoehoe that is not down this road is mostly mauka of the highway and goes up into the hills.

Homes, when they come on the market, vary a lot in price because of the vast differences in size, age, quality and lot-size. They are available here from time to time for a bottom of around $200,000 on up. The weather is best described as rainy. Even at the lower elevations, because of the East-facing cliffs, this area is nearly always damp. The lush foliage along the road to the ocean is good evidence of the wet climate.

From Laupahoehoe, shopping or any other town activity is a long drive in either direction.

There are other small communities on both sides of Laupahoehoe, and all offer widely varied properties. They range from tiny plantation cottages to elaborate estates.

Honomu

Only 12 miles from Hilo, this would be a nice place to live for folks who were going to work in town. Honomu likes to think of itself as an "artist's community," mainly because of the several excellent galleries along the short main street. It's a small community with only a few streets, but tiny homes do show up on the market here and they go for as little as $100,000. Expect to pay over twice that—or more—for a newer home on a large lot, though, because the lower-priced properties are usually ex-plantation homes on postage-stamp size lots. Some of these are really quite nice, though, and depending on your needs, they could serve you well.

This village, and the small commercial area, gets its traffic from the folks driving to Akaka Falls Park, only a few miles farther up the road. This is a small park with an easy one-mile walk through some spectacular scenery and to the viewing point of 400-foot-high Akaka falls. The quaint street lined with galleries and small eateries is on the road to the falls, so many of the tourists stop there along the way.

Papa'ikou

From Honomu to Hilo are several more communities. Pepeekeo, Papai'kou, and X are all in this area and have older homes available at affordable prices. You'll see newer ones there too, but the prices quickly transcend affordability. If an ocean view is not important to you, you can find newer homes that are still within reach. We've seen some great deals on nice places needing extensive repairs, too. If you have the skills and the inclination for this kind of project, tell your Realtor to find some "fixers" for you. Some Realtors routinely avoid even showing run-down homes to clients unless asked to do so.

Wainaku is very close to Hilo, so close that the lower portion is only a 10-minute walk from downtown. These are all worth your while to investigate if you feel comfortable with this kind of environment. It's semi-rural, and spotty in that there are some tacky places right in among the nicer homes. Many of these homes have great views of the beautiful Hilo Bay. Because of the fabulous views from the whole area, it seems to us to be ripe for upgrading. This has been happening in places like this, too. People start going in and buying a place here and another there, remodeling the worst ones, and pretty soon it catches on and the whole neighborhood cleans up. Of course, along with the clean-up come the escalated prices. If you're young, have lots of energy and can wait a few years to see the results, these areas make fine investments.

If you are attracted to this part of the Island but are looking for something a little more upscale, look for listings especially on the makai side of the highway, as this is where most of the nicer homes are. Again, you'll find small homes needing repairs right in there with the big, pricey ones. Some bargains can still be found in this area with a little perseverance.

Full Circle

Well, we're back in beautiful Hilo, so let's stop in at Bear's Cafe for an excellent cappuccino and some "talk story." We've gone all the way around this awesome Island now, and we've just touched on a few of the possibilities for affordable living. In between every two places we've visited, there are many more places hiding. Some, you'll never find no matter how long you live here, but the more you search, the more you'll discover.

We suggest that you collect your feelings about all the places you've visited so far, weed out the ones that you didn't care about at all, and slowly narrow your vision to a few locations. At that point, the only way you'll know where to call "home" is to spend some time in each remaining place. Feel the place—listen to your heart. Talk to people. Ask questions. Spend some time there at different hours of the day. See how quiet it is at night; how the ocean sounds from there. Be sure to drive every street nearby, too. Better yet, walk the area to get an even better feel of it.

Hilo Sunset   Camille Thomsen Photo

We once found this incredible home near Wainaku that we were ready to buy. We did our recommended drive all around every little nook and cranny and guess what we came across? A hog farm! The day we were there was windless (unusual) and this stinky hog farm was upwind of the place we were considering. The stench within a quarter mile of the farm was unreal, so we could only imagine how far it would have carried when the wind came back.

As we have already covered in "The Realities," other nuisances to look for are poultry or other kinds of farms, the tree frogs we mentioned earlier, or even some guy who is raising a yard full of roosters!. How would you like to wake up at five every morning to a hundred crowing roosters? And of course, unless you are a dog-lover and enjoy the sound of barking dogs, be ever vigilant for evidence of nuisance dogs. The signs include not only the dogs themselves, but kennels, dog runs, dog houses, and the ubiquitous local-style "tie-dogs." Tie-dogs are dogs kept on short chains at the corners of a person's property. There is usually a small shelter of some sort and the dogs, if they are serving their intended function, bark continuously, day and night. It is our recommendation to forget any property, no matter how desirable, if there are tie-dogs in the neighborhood. There is generally nothing that can be done to stop nuisance dogs in a neighborhood where most of the people don't find the noise to be a nuisance.

It is our feeling that the most important ingredient of your search should be to listen to your heart. After all the logical decision-making is over with and you think you have it all figured out, let your heart—your intuition—make the final decision.

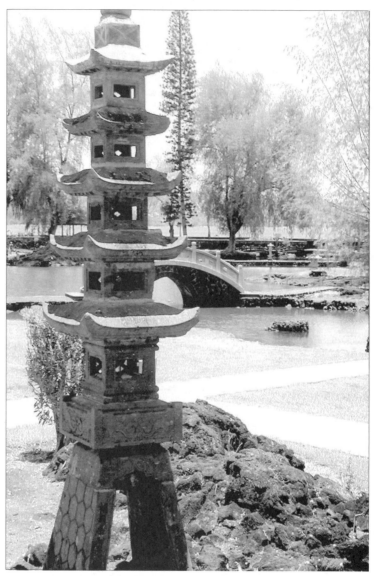

Liliuokalani Gardens, Hilo

Chapter Five

Making the Big Move

You've done the hard part. After a lot of thoughtful research, you've picked out the area of the Island where you want to live; you've decided whether to rent or buy and perhaps you've already chosen the exact house and tied up the real estate transaction. Now it's time to organize a smooth and easy transition to Paradise.

> Tip: On a pre-move visit to Hawai'i, be sure to pick up a Big Island telephone directory. It's an excellent resource for all sorts of useful information that will come in handy in planning your move. The phone book also has some of the best street maps you'll find anywhere, covering most areas on the Island. Phone directories are available at any of the "telephone stores" all over the Island.

In the Reference Guide in the back of this book, you'll find some recommended reading on the generic details of organizing a relocation move. We'll cover the basics here and then go into some detail on those things that make a move to an island in the middle of the ocean different from a move across the continent. If you feel a need for more detailed nuts-and-bolts info on moving in general, please check out our recommended titles.

The Plan

When you get all settled into your new Island home, you'll want to be thinking, "It's amazing how everything regarding this move just seems to have fallen into place. It's like it was meant to be." YES! That's the way it will be, and we're going to help the "falling into place" process with some planning tips.

The planning process should start at least a few months before your anticipated move. Matter of fact, the first thing on your list should be to decide the best time of year for the move. If you have school-age children, their timely arrival into the school environment—like between semesters—will be a consideration here. Weatherwise, it doesn't much matter on the Hawai'i end of your move, but the weather at your present home might be a big factor. Here, the weather is almost always moving-friendly, but the winter months do bring in storms and more rain. This will usually not present a problem for you, because your belongings will always be under cover except for the actual process of moving them from the shipping container into your new home. On the other hand, planning a move in winter from where the weather brings ice and snow might be asking for delays. Delays on one leg of shipping your goods can mean a missed connection at the following one.

The next thing you might want to do is decide how you will be shipping your possessions. Most people move their belongings to the Islands by way of shipping-container freight. A little later we'll discuss why some folks are sorry they did.

If you will be shipping a container-load of household goods, you'll need to get the container to your home for packing, and then from your home to one of the three shipping points to Hawai'i: Seattle, San Francisco or Los Angeles. From there the container goes on a big container-ship to Oahu, on a barge to Hawai'i Island, and then again on a truck to your new home.

We recommend Matson Navigation as your across-the-ocean shipper because we've had dependable and reasonable service from them, but there are others, as well, and you might want to compare prices before making a decision on this. You will want to call them for rates on full and partial containers, as this is a good starting point for determining how much you'll want to bring with you. Since the container will have to be delivered by truck to your present home for loading (by you or by hired help) and then moved to the freight docks, you'll want to get prices from several trucking firms. Check your yellow pages for options, and then call several and get an idea of their charges. Be certain you're comparing apples and apples, though, and make sure every rate you get is for the same services. For example, some freight rates are by the pound, while others are by the cubic foot.

Once you get these basic rates, you'll be in a better position to decide how much stuff you really want to take with you. Another real consideration in figuring your moving logistics is how far you live from the West Coast. If you are in the Midwest or farther east, it could cost you more to ship your furnishings to the West Coast dock than it will cost from there to Hawai'i. This is when it becomes necessary to do some careful planning on what—and what not to bring with you.

If you decide to bring enough of your household and personal goods that you will fill a container, it usually works like this: a trucking firm will bring the container to your home and you will be allowed a few days to pack it. (See "Packing and Unpacking Your Container" below.) Then it will be trucked to the nearest West Coast shipping dock, and from there it will travel by container-ship to Honolulu and from there by barge to Hilo. Another trucking firm will pick up the container in Hilo and take it to your new home, and again you'll be allowed a few days to over a week to unload it. When you have it all emptied out, the trucking firm will whisk it away and you will be officially moved in. Simple, huh?

It really is a lot less intimidating than it sounds. You will shop around for the best rate to haul your loaded container from your home to the shipping (Mainland-to-Hawai'i) docks, and then again from the dock in Hilo to your new home. We have a recommendation in the Resource guide for a good, dependable and reasonable trucking company on this end. They give you ten days to unload, too.

When getting prices from the trucking companies at both ends, ask how long they will leave the container for you. These times vary, and you'll want to try for as much time as possible. A week to ten days seems to be about the normal range of time, and a week should be the minimum you'll accept.

Packing and Unpacking Your Container

Long before the container arrives at your present home, decide on the best place for the trucker to park it. The first consideration is that the spot needs to be level or you'll have nightmares trying to stack and load boxes and especially heavy items. In some cases, it is possible to back the container close enough to the building to be able to use ramps from your porch directly into the container, making loading as easy as possible. Depending on your particular circumstances, it might even be feasible to remove a railing or other obstacle to facilitate ramps directly from the container into the house. Failing this luxury, make sure the trucking company supplies you with a long, sturdy ramp so you can easily wheel your heavy items into the container. Of course, all of these considerations apply at both your existing home and your new Island home.

Do not be tempted to use car-type jacks to level the container! Far better to check the location for level before the driver gets there and if necessary, level a spot in advance. Any dirt or gravel fill will have to be thoroughly compacted, though. Remember, that container can weigh up to five tons when loaded.

Another option if only a few inches of leveling is required is to have some sturdy planks available for the driver to back onto.

If you don't already own a hand-truck, you will want to ask the trucking company if they can supply one for you. If not, you'll have to rent or buy one yourself. Good hand trucks are actually inexpensive enough that you might consider just buying one, because after renting one at both ends you'll have pretty much bought one anyway, only you won't own it!

A tip: if you buy a hand-truck, don't go for the very cheapest because they are often flimsy and flexible enough to be dangerous. You don't need the most expensive one either, so go for the middle-of-the-road variety. "Home Depot" type stores (or even Ace Hardware stores) usually have good ones for around $40.

There are a few important "rules" to packing your container, whether you do it yourself or have somebody do it for you. One is to try your best to get as much stuff all packed and ready to go into the container as possible, but don't load any of it until you have it all ready to go. The reasons for this are that it's so much easier to pack efficiently if you have many different sizes of boxes and other stuff in plain sight to chose from, and also this allows you to make sure the first things in are the things you're the least likely to need right away when you get there.

Some people do better with lists. We are among them and can hardly function without them. If this includes you, start making your packing lists early and separate them into the items you'll need shortly after your arrival and the other things that you won't be needing right away. It's really inefficient and frustrating to have to scrounge through dozens of boxes and move tons of material several times to find the things you need. Those, by the way, will always be in the boxes at the bottom of the pile.

Another thing that helps a lot is to mark each box with its contents, or at least where the contents came from. For example, "dining room," "office," and like that. It's also helpful to mark each box on at least two sides so that the label will always be visible even when the box is still deeply embedded at the bottom of a huge stack of other boxes. You will end up moving some of your belongings several times before it's all done, but why do it more often than necessary? Let's plan to keep the work and frustration to a minimum.

In packing the container, it's important to pack it as tightly as possible. Keep all of your bedding available for padding between pieces of furniture. We kept all of our books available to fill small spaces, too. We would take a stack of books the right size and wrap them in a brown paper bag, and then use that package as a filler to keep things from shifting in the container. The less movement your packing allows, the less damage you'll get in your possessions. Remember, that container is going to be bounced down highways, picked up with cranes at the docks, loaded and unloaded into ships and barges, and floated across the ocean through whatever storms and rough seas nature has in store at the moment. Pack every nook and cranny, and even fill drawers and every other available space. You'll be glad you did when you get the container nearly full and there's still this big pile left to go into it.

Pack the heaviest items near the front (the doors are on the back) or in the middle of the container-not at the back. Of course, load the least-easily-damaged and the most crush-resistant items at the bottom and the most fragile at the top. Remember, you'll be stacking nearly eight feet high, and that puts a lot of weight on the things at the bottom of the load. The most important thing to keep in mind is to pack so that there can be no movement inside. Get a visual of this gnarly giant picking up your container and shaking it vigorously. Now pack so that nothing will bounce around inside when he does that, and you'll be fine. You'll know you did well when you unpack and there is nothing at all broken or damaged. A friend who recently moved over packed most of her belongings in commercially-available moving boxes of all the same size making loading the container much easier!

> Tip: the last things to go into the container should be the hand truck and any tools you might need to remove doors or other obstacles that can make unloading easier at your new home. Minimum tools would be a claw-hammer, hefty regular screw driver for removing hinge pins, a Phillips screwdriver and if there are any railings or the like that will need to come off, a small crow-bar.

Unpacking the container when it arrives is the fun part! After getting it as conveniently located as possible, carefully open the container doors, watching for anything that might have shifted in transit and is leaning against the door. This is when you will appreciate all the time you spent marking your boxes before you loaded them! Now you can have all those eager helpers take each box into the room where it will need to end up. If you have a big empty space somewhere, like a lanai, it's a good idea to stack the boxes you won't need right away in such a way that the labels are all readable. Try to stack the boxes against a wall but keep the stack only one row deep.

That way you'll always be able to see everything without having to move anything else first.

Be sure to leave yourself an ample path for any large items like furniture or appliances. Remember it takes a lot of room to navigate big pieces on a hand truck. Then when you get the last box out of the container, take a break and go jump in the ocean for a while!

What and What NOT to Bring With You

OK, now that you've got the container details down, let's talk about saving a whole lot of money and hassle by not even needing a container at all! There are a lot of things that are easy to replace here in Hawai'i and not cost-effective to ship.

Appliances and Other Big, Heavy Stuff

Appliances are big, heavy, hard to move and easily damaged in shipping, and cost about the same here as they do in most mainland areas. Unless your appliances are very dear to you and maybe you just bought them, you'd do better to leave them behind. You could either sell them at your mega-garage-sale, or include them in the sale of your house, if indeed you're selling your house. It is important to figure in the cost (and inconvenience) of all the shipping, packing and handling when figuring the cost-effectiveness of selling vs. shipping. In other words, don't just figure how much you feel your present appliances are worth compared to how much it will cost for new ones when you get here. To come up with a real figure you need to subtract all of the moving-related costs from their present value.

Example: You're considering bringing your washer, dryer and fridge. They're all about two years old and you paid $1400 for three appliances, so let's say they're worth $1000 now. Shipping them will add about $400 to your moving expenses, and new ones will cost you another $1400 in Hawai'i.

If you ship them over, your total investment in the three appliances will now be $1800 ($1400 purchase price plus $400 shipping). If you sell them for $1000 and replace them here for another $1400, your total investment will also be $1800 ($400 depreciation on the old ones plus $1400 purchase of new appliances). The bottom line is that the cost is the same, but if you sell them you've saved yourself a lot of hassle, plus you end up with brand new appliances again. And the new ones will most likely be delivered to your home for free by the store where you buy them. Obviously, this is just an example and the figures might not be representative, based mostly on the condition of your present appliances, but you get the idea. Another point in all this is that moving your appliances might just be the deciding factor in whether or not you even need to use a container. If it is, it becomes a lot more attractive to leave them behind.

Furniture and Other Household Goods

Furniture is not so easy a decision. For a lot of folks, a change to Island life inspires a change in home decor as well. For example, if you've been living with a houseful of heavy antique furnishings and this feels like the time to switch to a new, light, bright tropical ambiance, this is definitely the time to sell the antiques. Another consideration on antiques (or a lot of other wooden furniture) is that they often don't do well in tropical humidity. We've seen nice vintage furnishings come apart at the seams with the change in climate. Newer furnishings that use composition-board in their construction are also not very well suited for this climate.

With these things in mind, you'll have to decide if your furniture is special enough to you (like for sentimental reasons) to bring it along anyway. New furnishings tend to be expensive here, and there aren't a lot of choices in the way of stores. Hawai'i's itinerant population does, however, make for lots of garage and estate sales when people move back to the Mainland. Chapter 6 reveals the secrets of finding the best deals in new and pre-owned furniture.

As for the rest of your belongings, again, it's decision time and from here on in it'll be on an item-by-item basis. One extreme is to sell your home (if you are a home owner) furnished, or even partly furnished. You could sell it all, right down to the spoons in the kitchen, and start over when you arrive here. It all depends on what you have, how dear it is to you and what it would cost to replace it. We've known quite a few people who decided that since this is such a complete lifestyle change anyway, they would leave it all behind and start fresh here. Of course, if you are attached to the things you've been living with for years and would like to keep them in your life, by all means ship them over.

We'll just toss this in for consideration: We have some vacation rentals. We figure that it costs us right around $1000 to completely furnish a two-bedroom home with moving-sale furnishings, new bedding and bath supplies, and new kitchen appliances and utensils. The catch is that it might take a few months of going to sales to do the job, so if you use this method, don't expect to finish the job in a weekend!

Here's some food for thought: Among all the people we've talked to about this, there isn't one (including ourselves) who didn't say they brought over way too much and if they had it to do over they would have sold most of everything before moving. It really does simplify the move and cuts the costs to nearly nothing. If you pared your bring-along stuff to the minimum, you could actually bring some of it as check-in luggage and ship the rest in Priority Mail cartons. Each passenger is allowed two seventy-pound boxes, so for a couple, that's 280 pounds of stuff. Priority mail is expensive, to a point, but maybe not when you figure the charges are from your door there to your door here, and your belongings will arrive in a few days. Remember, shipping by the conventional means, your goods travel by truck to the West Coast docks, by container ship to Honolulu, by container barge to Hawai'i Island, and then again by truck to your door. The time enroute is from four to six weeks from your old home to your new one. Also, you are responsible for the arrangements with each of the shippers; it doesn't just happen automatically. We've talked to people here who did indeed ship a big pile (like a full pickup truck load) of boxes by Priority Mail and ended up paying a few hundred dollars instead of a few thousand—and all the attendant inconvenience—of shipping a houseful by container.

Clothing

Clothing might not seem like a big issue, but when you consider the amount of clothes the average person owns, it can become a big issue. Shipping all that stuff over here isn't the only thing, either; you'll find that because most folks here don't own or need a lot of clothes, closets are, by Mainland standards, diminutive. We pared down our clothing to what we thought was the basic minimum of necessities, and we still ended up taking most of what we brought to the local thrift shops. For even a couple, this can amount to some big boxes to ship, and if the goal is to make this move as economical as possible, then we need to ship as little as possible.

OK, what will we really need to bring? It depends on several factors, mostly on what climate you've chosen for your home here, and then your basic tastes in apparel. The first issue is easy. Unless you'll be living in the mountains, like Kamuela or Volcano, you won't need anything as toasty as a sweatshirt except for those rare occasions when you decide to go up to those frigid climes.

So what will you need here in the way of clothes? Just picture yourself living where the temperature rarely drops below 70 degrees. The days range from the low 70s to the high 80s, and the nights can drop into the 60s during the coldest months. The humidity is fairly high all year 'round, so cool, light clothes are in. Normal attire for most folks on most days here is shorts, a cool top or shirt and the traditional "rubber slippers." On the Mainland those slippers are also known as thongs or flip-flops. Most people wear the $2.95 disposable variety here, and for more formal occasions, one can step up to the $10 kind.

One good reason to adopt rubber slippers for your everyday footwear is the local custom of never, ever wearing shoes into a house. It is considered rude to wear shoes inside a home here, and it's a nice custom that's easily adopted, especially if you can simply kick off your slippers before entering somebody's home.

We still get a warm-fuzzy feeling coming to a friend's home for a party or other social engagement and seeing dozens of pairs of slippers in front of the door. The trick is to leave with the same ones you arrived in!

What about those "special occasions?" Even at the theater, a nice restaurant or at parties, people dress very casually here. By mainland standards, very, VERY casually.

You'll more than likely never have occasion to wear any of those dozens of pairs of fancy shoes again, and most of the clothes you used to consider as "casual" would probably now make sure everyone knows you're a malihini (newcomer) wherever you go. Perhaps the best way to decide what to bring in the way of clothes is to carefully observe what the folks who live here wear when you come on your next visit. You might be surprised!

Tip: Unless you are very attached to your leather goods, best not bring them to Hawai'i. This holds true anywhere in the Islands, too. Leather simply does not get along with the humidity here.

A scenario: You hang your expensive leather jacket in the closet and then a few months later you're going to a concert up in Volcano. Terrific! A chance to wear that old favorite jacket. Surprise! You get it out of the closet and it's all covered with a greenish-white furry mold. Yuk! After duly expressing your reaction to this sight, you get out some rags and brushes and spend half an hour cleaning every fold and crevice, only to watch it get even worse the next time it has to spend some time in the closet.

There is a cure, if you must keep leather goods. You can buy electric closet-heaters here to keep the humidity in your closets under control. They consume only about ten to twenty watts of power, but even so, if left on full time that can add a few dollars a month to your electric bill. The other option is to keep your leather in a very well-ventilated place that gets daily sunshine. Mildew and mold do not like sunshine in any quantity.

We've actually seen fine leather disintegrate if left in a tight closet long enough, so please consider giving all that leather to your best friend as a farewell gesture.

Your Car(s)

Should you ship your car? Only if it's very special, very dear to you, and if adding the shipping costs to what you have invested in the car still leaves you in a favorable position financially. Cars and trucks are not really any more expensive here than there. If you would like to see some real-time prices, on the Internet visit autotrader.com, enter the make and model of your (or any other) car, enter your zip code and search for ads. Then do the same thing only with a Hawai'i zip code. (Hilo is 96720.) Depending on where you live, the results might surprise you. Another way to find a representative cross-section of car prices here is to check the on-line classifieds in the Big Island's two newspapers. They're both listed in the Resource Guide.

Currently the rate Matson charges for shipping a car is pushing $1000 (depending on the size of the vehicle). Bear in mind, though, that this is the rate from the West Coast dock, so you'll also need to figure how you'll get the car to that point. There are vehicle-moving companies that will transport your car, and also "auto drive-away" companies who hire qualified drivers (?) to drive your car cross-country. You could also drive it yourself, of course, on your way to the airport. You just need to schedule your departure from either San Francisco, Seattle or Los Angeles and get a ride from the dock to the airport. Depending on where on the Mainland you live and the size of your family, this could save you a worthwhile chunk of your airfare to Hawai'i. You'll need to rent a car for a while, though, as the shipping can take up to six weeks. Car rentals are reasonable, though, and monthly rates are available. Another way to go, and one used by quite a few people, is to buy yourself an inexpensive car as soon as you arrive, and sell it when yours gets here.

About the only real advantage we can see in shipping over a car rather than buying one when you get here is that if you live in a very dry area where cars do not rust, you will be ahead of the game in that area. Cars do rust here, depending on your location and how you take care of them. Any day of the week, you'll see cars here that are so full of rust holes you have to wonder what's holding them together. Some of these cars might be only a few years old, too. Then on the other hand, there are lots of antique car enthusiasts here who have very old cars in like-new condition. They take car of their cars. We take reasonable care of our cars and one of ours at present is 13 years old and has no visible rust. The trick is we don't leave them parked right by the ocean, and when we do expose them to a lot of salt spray, we wash them with plenty of soap when we get home. Keeping your car well waxed helps, too.

Anyway, if your car is "just a car," and not something near and dear to you, we would recommend selling it and replacing it when you arrive here. Of course, all this presumes you're not going to "sell" your car to your dear brother-in-law for half of what it's worth and then pay full price for a replacement when you get here! If you get top dollar for your car there, you'll be able to replace it here for about the same price, again saving the nearly $1000, the bother of shipping it and the four-to-six week wait.

This is definitely going to be an adventure, and some careful pre-move planning can make it an enjoyable one.

Traveling Light

If you decide you'd like to sell nearly everything and travel light, you have several options. One, of course, is the All American Garage Sale. Everybody loves a garage sale, and you can sell a lot of stuff at a sale in the right areas. The right areas are those where it's easy for people to find you. The down-side of garage sales is that almost always, all the good stuff is gone in a flash and then you sit there for the rest of the day staring at boxes and boxes of trinkets, dishes, clothes and toys, all of which you will still own at the end of the sale. Bummer.

Here's a better idea: In your nearest-city phone book, look up "auctions." There are auctions all over the country that specialize in liquidating household goods. We've used these companies with a great deal of success on three occasions now. Believe it or not, the average price they got for our stuff at auction was at least double what we would have ever asked for it at a garage sale. They take their 30% off the top and you still win. Where you really win is that they sell everything, down to the last tiny item. They cleverly group all your little insignificant things into batches of items and the bidders have to bid on the batch. They always put some neat teaser in the top of the box, so if you want that item you have to buy the whole box. People go nuts at these auctions. It really is amazing. We've gone to watch a couple of them for entertainment after the last time they sold our stuff for us at unbelievable prices.

If you have some nice antiques, contact several antique dealers and find one who likes the kind of things you have and will take them on consignment. When we left the Mainland, we took a whole houseful of nice European antique furniture to a dealer and left it on consignment. For the next two years, we just kept getting these terrific checks in the mail for pieces they had sold— again for twice and sometimes three times what we would ever have asked for them had we sold them ourselves.

OK, if you've pared down the shipping needs to what you can take with you and ship by Priority Mail, you're that far ahead. If you've decided no, you would rather keep most of your houseful of furnishings, then we would like to remind you to consider carefully whether they will be appropriate to your new lifestyle. So often, we hear folks talk of the money they could have saved by not shipping over all the furnishings that they ended up replacing when they got here. Again, shipping or selling your present furniture and appliances can be the decision-maker in whether or not you need to bear the expense of using a container.

Last But Not Least: Taking Your Pets

For folks moving to Hawai'i and bringing pets, the whole quarantine issue and the huge fees charged for this service have presented a real problem. The separation of pet and owner for such a long time is even a bigger issue than the fee, and in come cases with older pets not able to cope with a month of quarantine, it has made the difference between moving to Hawai'i or not. This news should be welcome relief to an old and serious dilemma for many.

The new rule is effective June 30, 2003. Under this rule, pet owners have to arrange vaccinations and blood tests for their pets at least 120 days prior to their arrival in Hawai'i. The good news: Under the new rule, out-of-state pet owners would be able to arrive at Honolulu International Airport and leave with their pets within hours of their arrival.

This should be a very workable program, but you have to be prepared to plan ahead. The new fees will make pet owners moving to Hawai'i happy, too. The fee if your animal qualifies for a direct release from the airport will be $165, and $224 if it will require up to 5 days of quarantine. But the cost for a 30-day and 120-day quarantines will still be astronomical, at $655 and $1080, so it sure will pay to plan ahead and get your pet qualified for immediate release.

Pet owners who are still upset with Hawai'i's strict requirements to ensure that no animal with rabies enters the state might like to know that Hawai'i is the only rabies-free state in the nation.

Please check with the Quarantine for the latest updates, as this information is evolving rather quickly now, after many years of non-action and gripes from pet-owners.

If you need info on quarantine, please check the Resource Guide for complete access info for the Hawai'i Quarantine Station. They will send you the latest info packet, and it is important to get up-to-date information as the rules change from time to time-as do the fees. As of this writing, the fees for both dogs and cats is a whopping $555. For the 120 day quarantine, the fees are $1080. Also as of this writing, there is talk of dismantling the entire quarantine program. It seems that in the entire history of the program there has not been one single case of rabies and besides, there seems to be no medical or scientific justification for the quarantine or the insane fees.

Yes, it all seems very strange to hold up the folks who would bring loving and cared-for pets with them, when enforcement for strays and spaying is largely ignored here. It's a big decision, and a lot of it has to do with the age of your pets and how well they will be able to tolerate the time in quarantine. If there is an unpleasant issue in moving to the Islands, this is it. But it is getting better.

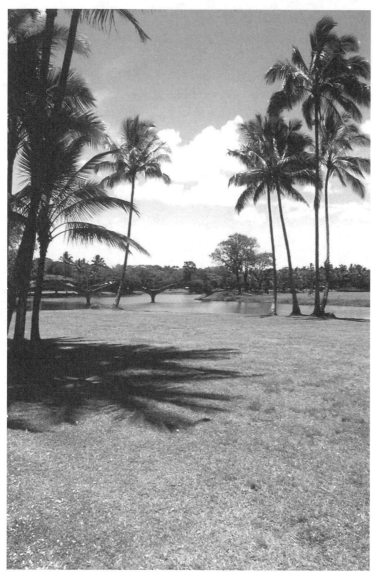

Wailoa Park, Hilo

Chapter Six

Shopping: Keeping the Costs Down

We often hear, "Groceries are so expensive in Hawai'i! How could I ever afford to feed my family?" We hear it over and over, and even from folks who have lived here for a while. They back up their claims by quoting one particular market's prices for milk, cereal and other packaged goods. Well, yes they're right. If you need to feed your family with imported, packaged, processed groceries, you will have a big food bill. But wait a minute . . . we're in Hawai'i! There are lots of farms here and we can buy fresh tomatoes and other delicious and nutritious produce year 'round!

We can buy a dizzying array of veggies and fruits at the local farmer's markets for half of what they cost at Safeway, and many of them are organic and they're all fresh. Fresh fish is available from some of the farmer's markets, from small local shops, from the grocery stores and even from the fishermen themselves right out of their coolers on their trucks alongside the road!

We do most of our shopping at the Hilo Farmer's Market. We also buy our fresh fish there or at one of the grocery stores if the price is right. Fish prices can vary from day to day depending on the catch, so we buy what there is the most of, which is usually the least expensive. We don't buy milk at one store for nearly $8 a gallon when we can buy it at any number of other stores for $3.79. We don't buy fish for $8 per pound when the catch is low, but when there's lots of it and the price is down to $3.50, we stock up. A freezer is a must here if you want to be able to shop effectively. We just have a small one, but it does the job well. Our total grocery bill is substantially less than it ever was when we were on the Mainland, and the food we get is a whole lot better. Ever taste one of those pinkish-gray, imported orbs they sell as "tomatoes" in the markets? At the Farmer's Market, the beautiful deep-red tomatoes were picked ripe that morning or the day before and are scrumptious!

There are other, more creative ways to obtain in-season fruits and veggies, too. Like instead of paying nearly $3 a pound for mangoes at the supermarket, we drive down to the Red Road in Puna and pick up as many as we can use off the ground. After you live here for a while, you'll likely never again pay for things like avocados, mangoes, pomelos (Hawai'ian-style grapefruit), lilikoi (passion fruit), guavas, or any of the other goodies that grow in abundance here. After a while here, you'll discover all the "secret" places where you can pick up all the fruit you want off the ground or even off of trees the owners don't care to harvest themselves. And even if you must buy at the Farmer's markets, how about papayas at five for a dollar? Or avocados at four for a dollar with several varieties to choose from. No, our groceries are not expensive.

We never have figured out the reason for the astronomical prices of boxed cereals here, except that as long as people keep buying them at those prices, I suppose the message to the suppliers is to keep supplying them at those (and higher) prices. If you insist on buying packaged, processed (not good for you anyway) foods, then get them at Costco in the huge sizes for about the same price as the little boxes at the supermarket.

We have Costco (in Kona), Wal-Mart, Home Depot, Lowes (Kona), and other Mainland-style outlets here for those who like that kind of shopping. Costco is a genuine savings on a lot of things. If yours is a big family and you have the freezer space, you will do well there.

The Big Rule of Hawai'i Shopping

The one Big Rule here is to shop around. We find that there can be huge price differences from one store to another for the same item. It doesn't matter what it is, either. Auto parts, hardware, appliances or groceries all qualify. We find it isn't uncommon to get price differences of 50% or more from one supplier to another. It really does pay to make a few phone calls before buying anything costing more than a few dollars. Another tip: There is no consistency to the price differences, either. One store may have your favorite laundry detergent on sale this month, and another will next month. Shop around, and watch the sale flyers in the newspapers.

Another Big Rule: if you find any non-perishable items you need on a regular basis and the price is right, buy a bunch of them! For various reasons that include shipping, storage and other factors, stores here do not manage their inventories like they do on the mainland. You can go into Longs Drugs and find your favorite shampoo, for example, at half of what you've been paying for it elsewhere. So you buy one and decide to remember next time you need shampoo, get it at Longs. Bad move. Next time you need shampoo, Longs might just not carry that brand any more. Same thing at Costco.

You go there and they have this terrific deal on HP printers. You tell yourself, well, I'm coming back here next week anyway, I'll pick up one then. And then next week they're all gone and the manager tells you sorry, no more.

It seems like a lot of attractively-priced merchandise here is a one-shot deal. So when you find something you need on a regular basis and it isn't perishable, stock up! Even if it's an exception and will continue to be available, it will cost more next month than it does today.

> Tip: If you find an item you really need at a great price, even if you were not planning on making the expenditure right now, go for it because it most likely won't be there when you need it.

Take Yourself on a Tour

When you have some free time, take a tour of your nearest (and even the not-so-near) shopping resources. Especially if you will be doing any decorating or remodeling, go visit all of the businesses that provide the things you might need: Hardware stores, building-materials stores, decorating shops, and even the department stores. Price structures are not the same here as on the Mainland, and you might be surprised at what you find. It's a good idea to have some general knowledge of what's available and who carries it if you are to become a frugal shopper here.

Tour the various grocery outlets, too, and get a general idea of overall pricing, inventories, freshness of goods, and just the feeling you get from the different places. Forget everything you've ever learned about shopping on the Mainland; the rules are all different here.

Be sure to find out where the farmer's markets are in your area and visit all of them eventually. Prices vary, especially in the more touristy areas. A general rule is that any markets easily available to tourists will have higher prices than those tucked away and harder to find.

Mail Order vs. Local Shopping

We rely on mail-order for a lot of the things we need, including tools, household goods and any number of specialty items. The Internet has made mail-order so much easier now, what with not even having to have a "real" catalog. You just go to your computer, type in whatever it is you need, and there it is, being offered by numerous vendors.

There is one condition to our shopping mail-order, though, and we like to encourage everyone to follow suit. Please give our local merchants and suppliers first chance at filling your needs. Often, it's just so easy to go to the computer and punch in a few keystrokes. A few days later, your treasure is in the mailbox. But we have lots of stores here whose owners and managers try their best to keep prices as low as possible, not to mention support their families. We always give them first chance and even if the cost is slightly higher, we'll buy local. One thing the slightly higher price will buy you is continued and friendly service should something go wrong. Dealing with defective merchandise bought on-line can be a real headache.

Shipping Costs

Be sure to include shipping costs when comparing prices between mail-order and local purchases, too. Remember that the shipping costs on heavy items can easily use up any savings in the cost of the item itself.

Speaking of shipping, when we order anything that weighs only two pounds or so, we've learned to ask up-front if shipping by Priority Mail is an option. If the vendor says no, we try somebody else. Consistently, items shipped to us by UPS or FedEx take longer to get here and cost far more. For example, UPS has a minimum charge of around $15 (depending on where the shipment originated on the Mainland), so if you're buying an item that costs $50 or less, that can add significantly to the overall cost. If the item is less than two pounds in weight, Priority Mail will get it here for $3.85 in a few days. FedEx or UPS will cost you their minimum of at least $15 and it could longer to get to you. One caution, though: with the new USPS postal rate hike in effect, the rate difference gets less and less as the parcel-weight increases.

And to be fair, we have received both FedEx and UPS shipments from the Mainland in two days, too, but this is clearly the exception.

Before 9/11, Priority Mail delivery time from the West Coast was usually two days and rarely more than three. Since then, the mail can no longer go on airliners as baggage, so it has slowed a bit. Now, we expect Priority Mail packages in three to five days. Hopefully, that situation will be rectified in the not-too-distant future.

We just received a package of books from Seattle that was shipped FedEx "overnight" and it took a week to get here. One of the reasons is that the FedEx drivers don't seem to know the rural areas and if they have difficulty finding an address they take the package back and send you a notice though the mail! So much for overnight. Actually there is no such thing as "overnight" to the Big Island (or any other outer Island). So-called overnight packages might make it to Oahu overnight, but from there they get shipped to the outer Islands the following day.

More on Shopping Local

Our dedication to shopping local extends to avoiding the big discount chains if we can do as well locally. Many of the Mainland biggies are represented here and more are showing up all the time. We have found, over and over, that these giants have some of their advertised goods priced well below the local competition, but the bulk of their offerings are often the same or even higher than local prices. Office Max in Hilo is a good example. We have two locally-owned office supply stores in Hilo and both consistently beat Office Max in a lot of their prices. Again, it comes down to shopping around. Shopping around does take some time and effort, but if getting the most out of your hard-earned dollars is important to you, you'll find your time is well spent.

It has been our consistent experience that most items can be purchased here for about the same as mainland prices, at the possible expense or inconvenience of not having what you want at the moment you want it. The trick is to buy when you see it at the right price instead of buying on impulse of what you feel you need at the moment. Planning ahead is a valuable tool in this process. Like if you know you're going to be redecorating your home in the near future, don't wait until the day you start the project to begin looking for what you need.

Keep the project in mind as you peruse the sales or browse the stores, and pick up whatever you find at a good price when you find it. Same goes for major purchases like appliances. If you know your washer and dryer are not long for the world, don't wait until one or the other dies and then expect to find a great deal on a replacement. As soon as you decide a replacement is due soon, start looking for the deals. We have the occasional lapse ourselves: We just bought a fridge for a rental a few weeks ago for $750 and this morning's paper listed the same exact item for $549! Ouch! In this case, it was a minor emergency. We had a few weeks notice on this one and shopped all the local sources for the best price. $750 was the best deal going at the time, so we grabbed it. So much for listening to our own advice . . .

For sure, don't make the mistake of taking a note of where you saw an item and then expect to find it there at the same price (or at all, for that matter) when you get around to needing it!

More on Shipping

You'll find some local merchants will automatically charge you a shipping charge on any items they need to order in for you. For example, you go to the appliance store and you look over the large selection of refrigerators. What you really want, though, is one with all the features of the almond-colored one, but in white. The salesman says, no problem, he can have one like that in the store for you in a week. But, he says, there will be a $50 shipping charge to get it here from Oahu. Forget that! There are more appliance stores on this Island, and they all love to sell their refrigerators. You will most likely find exactly what you want if you—anyone?—Yes! Shop around!

Then when you do find the exact one you want, try to contain your enthusiasm and be looking at a different one when the salesman approaches you. After he gives you the price on that one, shake your head in dismay and ask him how much for the ugly one—the one you really want. Rarely are prices here set in stone, even at such stores as Sears. You can almost always get the store to drop the price, even if only a little, with some creative applied sales resistance. Sometimes price-drops come in the form of free delivery. At the very least, get the store to deliver it for free!

The added shipping charge is often valid, but you can avoid it in most instances by finding what you want from somebody else. There's an art to confining your needs to what is available locally. Some folks pick up on this right off, and others fight it forever. Observing local traditions, tastes and styles and adapting them to your own lifestyle can save you a lot of money and frustration. The folks who have the most trouble are those who bring their mainland notions of how things should be done. Like the guy who decides to build a big Spanish-style house in a community of conservative local-style beach homes and then wonders how come he has trouble finding adobe blocks or help that knows anything about that style of construction.

Home Furnishings and Appliances

New furniture is expensive here, but then it is on the Mainland, too. At this writing, we have no true "discount" furniture stores here, and this would be an excellent business opportunity for anyone so inclined! Note that there are several stores that advertise themselves as "discount," "warehouse," or other catchy buzz-words, but in fact they offer the same prices as anyone else.

What we do have, however, is an itinerant population, so there are lots of moving and garage sales! You have to be prepared to get to there early for the best stuff, but we've seen some terrific deals at these sales. There are a few outlets that deal in surplus hotel furniture, and these are the suppliers of choice for those who have to furnish vacation-rentals here. We've furnished three vacation-rentals very nicely from a combination of garage sales and used hotel furnishings.

Used hotel furnishings are not junk, either. Well, some are, but there are some five-star hotels here and when they replace furnishings, they usually replace all of it and upgrade the entire hotel, meaning that there will be some nearly-unused items in each lot sold. We've bought king-size beds at one of these places, for example, that look and feel like new, and they go for around $125 complete.

Again, watching the sale flyers in the papers will find you some bargains. The furniture stores do all run occasional sales, and that's the time to buy new.

One more source for new furniture at a discount is the occasional warehouse sale. Some of the dealers will from time to time bring in a huge container load of furniture, usually from Indonesia, and then rent a warehouse to run a "sale" until the supply is gone. Watch the papers for these, and know your prices before you assume that just because they're selling out of a container they are selling cheap.

Hilo does have several shops that specialize in imported furniture, usually bamboo, rattan, teak or some combination. Some of the stores are outrageous in their prices but others are very reasonable. Again, take the time to shop around.

For some reason, appliances don't seem to be higher here than on the Mainland. Out of a recent Sunday-Paper Sears ad: A new 18-cubic-foot fridge for $516, a premium washer and dryer for under $700 for the pair, a dishwasher for $260, and any number of new ranges starting at under $400. These prices are representative of any number of appliances stores. There are also several places that sell refurbished and guaranteed appliances for really cheap prices. And again, you can find appliances at garage sales, too.

One caveat on appliances: depending on your location on the Island, many appliances will rust out before they wear out, so buying used means you need to scrutinize for rust. Look at the backs of washers, dryers and ranges, and the tops of the cabinet and doors of refrigerators. That's where the rust usually shows up first.

The same goes for furniture, too. Especially if you will be living anywhere near the ocean, don't even think about buying outdoor furniture made of steel! Pay the few extra dollars and make sure it's all aluminum. Take a small magnet with you when you shop and if it sticks to anything on the furniture (even if it's advertised as being made of aluminum), it is steel and it WILL rust.

Indoor furniture, especially items like futon frames, are often made entirely of steel. You would be much better off with one made entirely of wood. If you must buy furnishings made of steel, like perhaps a hide-a-bed in which the entire mechanism is made of steel, make sure the joints and connections are all lubricated on a regular basis, or one day when you need to open it for a guest it might just be rusted shut!

Tip: when you unpack your new (or newly-moved and rust-free) appliances, apply a coat of good-quality automotive paste wax as soon as possible, and then repeat the process once a year. This makes a big difference in how long they'll last before the rust starts to show, especially on the tops of the fridges and their doors. Top surfaces of everything seem to show rust first, so keep them as well protected as you can. Of course, had the manufacturers applied a decent coat of paint at the factory or made even the teensiest effort at rust-protection, this wouldn't be necessary. In these days, however, it isn't considered good business to manufacture goods that will last longer than the warranty period, so we must take whatever steps we can to preserve them ourselves.

Stereos, TV's and other entertainment units are no more expensive here than on the Mainland, so unless you have some very nice and nearly new equipment, you might do better to sell it and replace it with new when you arrive. Electronics equipment doesn't like high humidity, and the first thing that seems to go in your entertainment equipment is the speakers. The foam rubber "surrounds" that hold the speaker cones into their frames seem to simply evaporate in short order. Some will last for years, but others will need repair or replacement in months. A lot depends on their exposure to the elements, so it's good to position your speakers (and electronics) where they do not get any direct breezes from outside. This is particularly important in the rain-forest areas where the humidity is the highest.

Another tip: There is a product known as "ACF-50" that really works to stop corrosion. It's expensive, but the $15 spray-can goes a long way if properly applied. I found out about it in aircraft use years ago and have been using it with success around the house and on computer equipment. It's highly recommended and the manufacturer also has another product called "Corrosion Guard" which appears to be identical in performance. Check the Resource Guide for a source.

Computers and office equipment fall into the same category as electronics. We have learned to keep a dehumidifier in our office and that helps a lot. Actually, we recently discovered that a small, efficient air conditioner does a better job that a dehumidifier and it cools the room as a bonus. We had originally opted for the dehumidifier thinking it would cost less to run, but that was not the case. We recommend Panasonic room air conditioners, and don't buy one any bigger than necessary.

Normally, we never opt for "extended warranties," but here we have learned to buy them on computer equipment. There are numerous excellent computer businesses here that sell and service computers and peripherals at very competitive prices. It has been our experience that there is usually a very small (if any) difference in price between locally-supplied and mail-order computers and peripherals. If you factor in shipping costs and the convenience of having local support, this is an excellent case for shopping local.

On the flip side, we've got two Dell computers in our office and they have been serving us very well. We stopped having computer problems once we dried out the office. In addition to our now-dependable computers, our printers and all other office equipment work better and last longer. Paper is nice and dry now, so no more paper jams in our printers.

Vehicles

Like anyplace else, pre-owned cars are usually best bought from individuals rather than from dealers. For any given make, model and year vehicle, you can usually find it from a private party for way less than at any dealer, and then you save the mind-numbing experience of being put through the dealer's "system sell," not to mention the taxes and all the other creatively-inspired fees and charges. You can safely figure that a $5000 used car from a dealer will cost you an additional $700 by the time you get it out the door, most of that being the aforementioned fees and charges. And of course, you could have bought the same car for $4000 from a private party in the first place.

Car shopping here isn't much different from anywhere else, except that you need to be wary of rust that for one reason or another doesn't show. Any late-model car that is advertised as having "new paint" is suspect. Examine the car in all the places where rust shows up first and see if you can find any signs of repairs there. Look at the bottoms of the doors, around the edge of the roof, the windshield posts, around the back window and edges of the trunk (inside the trunk, too), and be sure to look under the hood. If the outside of the car looks great but things under the hood are all corroded and rusty, it's likely the whole car looked bad before it was painted. Of course, if you are going to be living near the ocean where any car will rust soon, you might not care about visible rust as long as the car is in good shape mechanically. You can get some very good deals on cars like that because most people will reject the car when they see the rust.

Beyond this, use the cautions you would normally use when buying a car, and remember to never believe anything a car salesman tells you! There is a popular notion here that since this is an island and the dealers must rely on repeat customers to stay in business, that they are more likely to treat you fairly here than on the Mainland. This has not been our experience nor that of most of the people we've talked to. Yes, there are some dealers here who have good reputations and who really do treat customers as though they expect to see them again when it's time for the next car purchase. You can find these dealers by asking around. Ask folks who have lived here for years and when the same name comes up a few times, that's your dealer.

Of course, this assumes that you would still rather pay more for the same car than you would have to with a private-party sale. Don't forget to add the 4% State Tax plus the $500-up in fabricated charges that you'll have to pay a dealer on top of the price you settle on. A fairly new trend is for dealers to charge a $200 "document fee" on every sale. There is no such legitimate thing as a document fee. It is merely one more way the dealer gets to extort an additional $200 from every customer. A "document fee" is not unlike Sears charging you $20 to write up the receipt when you make a purchase from them.

Another gimmick some of our local dealers have been using is a charge for a "theft deterrent package" that just happens to already be on the vehicle you're interested in, so you have to pay for it. The so-called theft deterrent amounts to some marks that were supposedly put on the windshield so that it and/or the car itself can be identified in case of a recovered theft. I've looked at some of these vehicles and could not find any evidence of any marks on the windshield, nor does the whole concept seem valid.

It's too bad that some car dealers seem to work hard to make sure that all car dealers keep their lousy reputation. Private-party sales are still the way to go.

Many people assume that they are better off buying from a dealer because they can get a warranty. Dealers offer "warranties" only on those cars that they are almost certain will not need them. And the "warranty" is not a warranty at all, but rather an insurance policy that you pay dearly for. If you do not buy the policy, you have no more warranty on your purchase than you do from a private party. Matter of fact, you have less, because a private seller with some integrity might work with you on a problem that happens shortly after you buy the car, but when you buy from a dealer, you will be signing a document (the "FTC sticker") that clearly states you are buying the car "as-is," with no guaranties, either implied or stated. This document even states that you acknowledge that nothing the dealer or salesperson tells you is necessarily true. Does that make you feel safer about a dealer purchase?

Clothes, Etc.

Depending on your personal tastes and needs, your can cut your clothing budget to near-nothing here. In the first place, there is no need for "seasonal" attire. It's summer year 'round. See "Clothing" in Chapter 5 for more on this topic.

The Bottom Line(s)

In conclusion, let's say one more time that the most important ingredient to keeping costs down is to shop around. On any items worth more than a few dollars, never accept the first price you get. Of course, the first one might just be the cheapest once in a while, but what are the odds? Prices vary for many reasons, not limited to supply-and-demand, inventory on hand, promotional sales, and brand names.

Sometimes, some of the bigger stores will make huge purchases of a few popular items and because they got them at a rock-bottom price, they will offer them as a "leader" to get people into the store. Some of the stores do this as a regular practice and once you're in the store after that single on-sale item, take notice of the rest of the prices. They might just be higher than any place else. Keep your eyes open, know what the prices are before making significant purchases. Don't assume that because a particular store has some good advertised prices that everything there will be reasonable.

Please try to shop local first. If you can find it at a locally-owned store, buy it there. Help support our local merchants, because every time the biggies put another one of them out of business, they can then raise their prices accordingly. And they do. We try to keep current on the prices of things we need on a regular basis and we have noticed that some of the huge Mainland-owned "SuperStores" have consistently higher prices than some of our local shops. It's their advertised specials that draws in the crowds.

216

Again, when you find a good price on non-perishable things you know you'll be needing, stock up! You might never get that price again. With a little practice, you'll get your cost of living to a minimum and enjoy doing it.

Distant views on the Kona Coast are often partially obscured in volcanic haze (vog).

Chapter Seven

Income Opportunities

You may have heard that it's next to impossible to find work here. NOT! Well, let's qualify that. If you come to Hawai'i and go to the State Employment Department to ask for a job, there isn't likely to be much of a selection. In the first place, there aren't that many jobs available, and when one does come up it will more likely go to a local than to a newcomer, as well it should. But there are lots of income opportunities available to those who do not need a boss to tell them what to do next, and there are jobs available to those who excel at whatever it is they do.

> News Flash: At this time, Hawai'i is the Number One State in low unemployment. Compare that to the rumor that there are no jobs in Hawai'i!

Here's the Big Secret: The one thing that is in short supply here is competence in nearly any field. Which is not to say that you can't get anything done competently here; there just isn't enough competence to fill the need. If you know how to do something really well and you're a dependable person willing to sell your time at a reasonable rate, there is no shortage of work. We know of no one who has a marketable skill who is looking for work. Quite the contrary; most people have more work offered than they have time for.

The job market is better now than it has been for many years. Most of this is because of the huge numbers of people who have recently decided that Hawai'i is the address to have. Along with large increases in population, there is always a new need for help in just about every field. The "help wanted" listings in the local newspapers confirm the need, as there are now three times the number of listings there were only a year ago, plus many of them are for mainstream positions with all sorts of companies.

Of course, any area of construction has the biggest and most consistent need for help. So much so that some contractors are offering to train workers. A really good, all around carpenter can now ask for $35/hour and get it in a heartbeat.

The high-tech sector (mostly in communications) has discovered Hawai'i Island's ideal climate and (relatively) cheap real estate, and there are more companies coming in all the time. Because East Hawai'i is now the fastest-growing area of the State, the new population growth dictates the need for more housing and services, and with that, even more jobs.

Very often, we hear from somebody who is about to move back to the mainland and when we ask why, it's always the same answer: "Can't find any work here." But when we ask these people what kind of work they do, the answer is usually something like, "I'd do anything that pays a decent wage." In other words, they have no specific marketable skills; they just want "a job." These are the people who have trouble finding work and who have helped perpetuate Hawai'i's "no jobs" reputation. It's unfortunate that many parents here do not encourage their kids to have developed a marketable skill by the time they get out of high school. Many don't even have an interest, let alone a skill. For them, yes, it is hard to find work. It's not just the kids, either. We hear the same thing from adults who come move over here hoping to find work. The ones who are willing to take any kind of a job because they have no particular skill, training or the desire to create their own jobs are the ones who eventually return to the Mainland because "there is no work here."

A young man we recently spoke with is an example "creating jobs." He told us he was leaving for the Mainland soon, because after nearly a year of looking for work he was convinced it isn't going to happen. I asked him what kind of work he's looking for and he said he'd take anything. Further questioning revealed that he was a skilled landscape person and had worked in this field for years. We offered that there are hundreds of home-owners here who stay for a few months and live on the Mainland the rest of the year, and that he could probably keep as busy as he wanted to just doing landscape and yard maintenance for them. He made it clear that he had no interest in doing this on his own. Rather, he wanted "a job." This is a good example of what it takes for many to make it here. If you have what it takes to find a need and fill it, you will not be looking for work long. If you need a conventional job, it is much more difficult.

Consider the benefits available to the young landscape person. Working for somebody else, he has to do whatever comes along. He will be, in many cases, unable to express himself with his own special talents. He will get a wage of approximately half of what his boss charges the customers. The flip side: Working for himself, his hours are his own, his tools and equipment and all other expenses are deductible, his income is directly proportional to his effort, skill and creativity and he gets to pick and choose the jobs he wants and the days on which he chooses to do them. Food for thought.

How about this: We have some vacation rentals. We pay our garden-person $40 every two weeks to mow the lawn at each one. He spends about an hour doing an excellent job of mowing, trimming edges and cleaning up after himself. He works all day, every day, at similar jobs and we had to look hard to find this guy!

When the garbage disposal went out at a rental a few weeks ago, we called the handyman who fixes things like this for us and for many others. He went out and replaced the unit. It took him one hour, he charged us $60. We felt it was a good deal for both of us.

There are "help wanted" ads for everything from dental assistants to scientific positions at the several world-class telescope operations atop Mauna Kea. There are ads for laborers, skilled "blue-collar" workers, professionals in many fields, and even orchard workers.

Again, all that's needed to find work in Hawai'i is some kind of a marketable skill and the willingness to work. Anyone who tells you any different isn't serious about working.

Bring Your Hobby

A lot of retired folks here have hobbies or part-time businesses that bring in some income to supplement their retirement. Some folks we've met who have no regular retirement income have simply continued long-standing hobbies and turned them into small businesses. Others have continued whatever it was they did for a living, only scaled down to a greatly reduced pace.

We know a lot of retired folks here and we don't know of too many who spend their retirement years sitting in the proverbial rocking chair. There are just too many fun-and profitable-things do to with one's time.

Some Fields of Opportunity

We've got friends who are woodworkers and are as busy as they wish to be (sometimes busier) trying to keep up with the demand. One neighbor makes clay jewelry in her home, just sold her beautiful, paid-for home on 3 acres and is building an even nicer home now (for cash), her car is paid for, she lives well and salts away money every month.

Another neighbor opened a gallery nearby and sells the work of selected Island artists and craftspeople. She has expanded her gallery several times in the last few years and is doing very well. Her husband makes classic Island-style and exotic furniture (lots of it!) out of Koa, a beautiful indigenous Hawai'ian wood, and is always behind in his orders.

Others include (very) successful photographers, fine-artists, writers, farmers, fishermen, builders, treetrimmers, home designers, cabinet-makers, B&B owners, house-cleaners, yard-maintenance and landscaping business-owners, and owners of various stores, restaurants, and other small businesses.

There are folks doing well with massage, counseling, at-home computer-based businesses, auto repair, and then there are the professionals who come here and continue their professions but at a much-reduced pace. Right now, this whole Island is in dire need of a few good, reliable cleaning services to take care of the quickly-growing vacation-rental business.

Yard maintenance is another field needing capable workers. And remember, this is a tourist-destination, and although this side of the Island gets fewer tourists than the Kona side, there are still enough that there are lots of opportunities serving that population. Along that line, there's even a market here for good musicians!

A note on the tourists here, the ones who come to the Windward (Hilo) side of the Island usually have different expectations and needs than do those who go to Kona. The less-typical tourists who visit the rural and green side are more interested in things and activities that involve exploration, the arts, culture, and a non-commercial experience.

There's a whole different-and interesting-market in serving folks who shy away from the typical busy tourist scene.

An opportunity that's fairly unique here is house-sitting! There are always folks who need to travel to one place or another and need dependable care of the home and possibly pets while they're away. And there are the "snowbirds," the people who own a home here and one on the Mainland and stay here during the winter months. Some of these folks prefer not to leave their homes vacated when they are away.

These arrangements are from short-term, like a week or two, to many months. Someone with a good reputation in this field would seldom be looking for a position. This might also be the ideal setup for those who would like to live in different places all over the Island before settling on "the right one." And then the house-sitting opportunity has spawned another opportunity, as well. This happens a lot here, and creative people are starting new, innovative and successful businesses all the time. The new one here is for somebody to make up a database of people seeking and needing house-sitting services and then to connect them for a reasonable fee. Connecting people with their needs is one of the fastest-growing and most successful small businesses around, and all that's needed is a computer and a phone line. See "Some More Opportunities," below.

No work in Hawai'i? Give me a break! We do remodels and in the last few years we've been trying hard to evolve this business into one where we (my Bride and I) do less and less of the actual physical work. The trick is in finding anyone else to do it! We've spent lots of time trying to find help in the areas of plumbing and wiring repairs, tile-setting, general carpentry, and even interior painting. Sure, we've found a few people who said they can do the job, but sadly, the reason they were available is because of their incompetence. We've hired guys who said they were master carpenters and whose work would scarcely qualify them to build packing crates. We've hired a number of "painters" whose expertise was limited to knowing how to get some paint out of a bucket and onto a wall. One of our "plumbers" installed a horizontal drain line that ran uphill! And most of these people are charging $25-35 per hour!

We have been fortunate to find a few helpers who are both competent and dependable. We treat them very, very well. There is lots of work available here for those who can do it.

Staying in Business

There's a saying here: "Big Island; small world." Word travels fast here, and anyone who performs his or her service with competence, dependability and integrity will get a reputation in a hurry. The laid-back Island lifestyle encourages what might appear as a flaky business attitude, so anyone who has a strong work-ethic here will be in demand!

Remember the story of the contractor who didn't show up when he said he would because the surf was particularly good that day? Here's a variation on that one, this time for an estimate for a job, and for a specific time of day rather than a day of the week. You've been told the guy will show up at three o'clock.. He shows up alright, but at five minutes to four. Well, in Hawai'ian time, if it isn't four yet, it's still three! Really! And when you think about it, it makes sense . . . kind of.

You get his price quotation, it's very reasonable and you feel good about his competence. He says he'll start tomorrow. Well, you're assuming now that because he'll start tomorrow and he said the job will take three or

four days, he'll be done in three or four days, right? Not exactly. He might start tomorrow . . . and he might not. It's a surf thing. But don't be surprised if it's two weeks before he's finally done with the job.
Remember, he said "three or four days," not necessarily consecutive days.

You can usually avoid this type of thing if it's really important to you that a job be done by a certain time. You have to make that very clear up front, and some people will accept it and do the job and others will simply tell you they don't work that way. Fair enough, right?

This is like a different country and the above scenario is more the rule than the exception. It is entirely normal and expected. This scene, of course, is a generalization and it doesn't always come off this way. Sometimes people actually do exactly what they say they'll do, and even do it on time. And they, you'll find, are the ones who are never out of work.

What your trade or profession happens to be doesn't matter. There are few skills that are not needed here just as they are on the Mainland, and although there are not always a lot of "jobs" being advertised as available, there is always a demand for skilled help. That may seem like a curious statement, but what it boils down to is that the person who has a skill and the self-discipline to be able to work on his or her own is the one who will make it here. It's the need to work for somebody else that presents a problem. There aren't a lot of employers because many of the small businesses here are so small that they run quite well with the help of a few friends or family members.

This is changing, what with the new businesses of all sizes moving here. The Hilo side population is just now getting to the level where it is attracting the attention of those kinds of businesses plus inspiring local folks to open new businesses, too.

The University of Hawai'i, Hilo Campus is growing by leaps and bounds, and there are constantly new positions opening there. The telescope operations in Hilo and on Mauna Kea are growing and need high-tech-capable people.

If you are fortunate to be the master of a number of skills, you would do well to check around in the area of your choice to see what skills are needed there. And do consult the "help wanted" sections of the local papers if you're looking for any kind of professional placement. There aren't many offerings on any particular day, but they do come up on a regular basis. Dropping off resumes at businesses that seem attractive to you is another good approach. Remember, Hawai'i is a "people place," so drop them off in person.

Word travels fast on an island. If you're good at what you do, you'll soon have more work than you want. There is always a demand for the people who get a reputation for competence and dependability.

The Arts

We've amazed several of our visiting mainland artist friends when we introduced them to our friends here who are supporting themselves quite well with their art.

The more common scene on the mainland is that artists must have a "real job" to support their art!

The arts and crafts field is alive and well here and supports many people quite nicely. The ones who seem to do the best are those who have developed a genuine feel for Hawai'i, her people and her magic. Their art reflects this feeling and when it comes through as genuine, it sells well not only to tourists, but to locals as well.

It's interesting to go to some of the many events that feature crafts booths and look at the offerings. After doing this for a while, you can get a clear picture of what sells well and what does not. Quality and craftsmanship are definitely important, and the buying public does know the difference! It is also interesting to see all of the innovation and creativity displayed at these events. Just when you think there can't be any more original ideas, you'll be surprised with some more.

Here's yet another opportunity related to the arts field. We know of several artisans and writers who would jump at the opportunity to have somebody represent them and their work at the many galleries and other outlets around the Islands. Sales and promotion have always been huge obstacles to success for artists, writers and crafts people. Most do not have the time, expertise or the inclination to handle their own promotion and distribution, so their work often stays unsold. Simply getting it out there, exposing it to the many venues available here, would make all the difference.

We also know of one very successful photographer who makes his own trips to all of the galleries and shops that handle his work on all of the Islands. He does this because he has not been able to find anyone who will represent his work in a manner consistent with his needs. His needs are simple: a bright, enthusiastic person who is both dependable and trustworthy. There are not even any sales involved here; just doing the rounds to check inventories and to help the various merchants with their restocking orders. A commission of 25% would be reasonable to pay for this work, plus additional commissions for any new accounts. Who would be your clients for this kind of service? A big percentage of all the artists and crafts people in Hawai'i. Of course, this would only work for somebody who would enjoy making monthly tax-deductible trips around the Islands.

Even good musicians do well here! Remember, we have a largely tourist-based economy here, and tourists just love to be entertained. There are also night-life spots that are frequented mostly by locals, and some of them feature live music, as well.

Opportunities abound!

Some More Opportunities

We also know of several people who have made successes of computer-based home businesses. They simply found different people who had a need to be connected, and they became the liaisons. We know of a woman who started an Internet vacation-rental listing service, and before her first year in business, she had over 1000 listings. She charged a very-affordable $100/year to her clients, put each listing on an attractive Web page, and that's all she needs do from there on in. She collects $100/year from each client each year for the continued listings, the clients are thrilled to receive world-wide advertising for their rentals for such a low price, and everybody is happy. She now has several thousand listings at $100/year . . . do the math!

There are always folks around who need their personal computers but are helpless when it comes to fixing problems, installing software, doing upgrades or any number of other tasks. If this sounds like yet another business opportunity, you're catching on!

There are lots of businesses here, ranging from very small to pretty darned big, and all of them rely on computers to do their business. Most of these businesses do not have staff computer tech people but have to rely on others to do their setup and maintenance work. Here's an opportunity for the person who has some real network skills.

Above, we mentioned the possibility of connecting house-sitting people with others needing their services. Once a core business is established on this Island, it can easily be expanded to the other Islands as well, and from there to other vacation destinations around the world. Think of the perks: deductible vacations around the world to check out new sites for development of your business!

Another friend runs aquarobics instruction at a local public pool and at a close-by huge, geothermally-heated tidepool. Not a bad way to earn a living! The tourist trade here also brings us other options, including vacation-rental needs ranging from the rentals themselves to management, booking and maintenance (badly-needed, too); wedding co-ordinators and related businesses; and of course, food service opportunities that are limited only by one's imagination.

A Story

This morning my bride, Camille, was on the phone with a young woman somewhere on the Mainland. Camille was ordering something out of a catalog, and when the woman took down our address, she started in on what was it like to live in Hawai'i, and then all the subsequent questions. She told Camille that she was in administrative work and would she be able to find work here? Well, because we get these kinds of questions often, we tossed around how we could address this topic in the book. What we came up with was that most of the people we know who are in administrative work seem to be doing it as a means to an end rather than as a vocation of choice.

Many administrative positions pay well, especially in the big cities, and the pay is the reason for being there. Many of them also carry more than their share of responsibility, headaches and heartaches. It seems somehow out of alignment to us, then, to think of coming to this place of peace and magic and to bring along such a stressful lifestyle-unless, of course, it is something that you genuinely enjoy doing.

One of the big problems with many administrative or even executive positions is that there is never any sense of completion. This isn't just an accident, either, but is designed into many such jobs. The corporations know that when they get an employee with a strong work-ethic who is driven to succeed, that person will respond in a predictable manner to a job with no sense of completion. The result is often an employee who will work extra hours for no extra pay, all in a never-ending passion to excel at a job in which there are no wins. The job never ends, it never comes to a point where the employee can kick back and feel good about his or her accomplishment. Whatever he or she does is never quite enough, and the rat-race goes on until there's a breakdown of some sort.

To those of you who are just doing it because it pays well, we would like to respectfully recommend considering changing careers! Scary? Yes, maybe it is. But we'd bet that the more thought you give the idea, the less intimidating it will feel.

Whatever you job or vocation is, if it's something you're doing only because the pay is good and you'd really prefer doing something else, do it! We've known doctors and highly-paid executives who have given up a lucrative practice in exchange for some serious inner peace in the form of a simple lifestyle of love and harmony with nature. We've also met some who have simply given up a busy and hectic big-city practice, moved here and started a limited, part-time practice that they could pursue with a glad heart. Then they could focus more on their clients or patients and life became better and more meaningful for everyone involved.

Eliminating stress from one's life is in itself healing.

Among the perks of downsizing your profession are the end of a big staff payroll and the attendant insurance and other headaches and overhead. Here, the lifestyle is so different from "big city" that the costs dwindle to a manageable amount, leaving the same net income with a lot less gross income.

Even the costs of having one of those high-paying jobs in the big city are significant. Consider the new car, the fancy clothes, the time spent commuting, social obligations—it all adds up. All of a sudden you can work close to home—or maybe even at home. Your commuting costs have gone away, your clothing budget is now nearly zip, you now have the time you used to waste sitting in traffic to spend with your kids (or at the beach), and you don't need the Lexus any more.

We always like to suggest that in choosing a career or even just a job, it is much better to decide first what fulfills us—what we enjoy doing, and then find work in that area rather than following the more usual approach of "going where the money is." After all, what we're all after in the end is peace of mind and happiness. Very few people who work just for the big bucks have much of either.

About That Lexus

The fancy-car thing is another interesting phenomenon here. On the Mainland, people tend to make assessments of our station in life, our credibility and more, by the vehicles we drive. And of course, on the long commute to work, we pass by innumerable conspicuous offerings of shiny new cars, constantly reminding us that what we have is not quite good enough. Being well-trained consumers, this influence tends to work, too. When we arrive at work we have to park amongst all the shiny, impressive new cars and we certainly can't be outdone there, either.

Here, nobody cares what you drive up in. Whether you show up in a Mercedes Limo or a rusty old pickup simply does not matter. It's hard for a lot of newcomers to get this, but sooner or later, even those most dedicated to their image tend to shed that feeling, and best of all, it's really a psychologically and spiritually healthier place to be.

"Where the Money Is"

We talk to friends and relatives who live in the Silicon Valley, California, one of the most expensive places in the country to reside. We ask them why is it so important to them to live in a place that is so hopelessly overcrowded, so incredibly expensive; where the smog is so thick it's hard to see buildings a few blocks away and the lifestyle is so frenetic; where sirens scream and tires screech, horns blare and car-alarms are going off everywhere, where car-jacking and road-rage are normal, where most conversation centers around stock options and where nobody seems to have time for anything worthwhile? The universal answer? "THAT'S WHERE THE MONEY IS!"

OK, let's do some simple math here. We know a few couples there who have to bring home well over $100,000 a year just to pay the expenses. No frills, just the bills. To bring home $100,000 after taxes, they need a combined gross income of far more than that. So they both have to work at full-time jobs so they can afford to live "where the money is."

We also know families who live very comfortably here in Paradise on $35,000 a year, and they make it with one income and have lots of free time to spend with family and friends, at the beach, going on trips, whatever. And many of the families here will be living in homes much nicer than those in the most expensive places in the country to live.

It's all in one's priorities, it seems. It's always been our feeling that it is essential to first find the place where you would like most to live, and then figure out how to support yourself there. Most folks tend to go where they think they can earn the most money, and then try to figure out how to be happy there. Unfortunately, the places with the traditionally high incomes are also the places with the traditionally high cost of living, the most crime, pollution, traffic problems and other elements interfering with one's peace.

Another Little Story

Our dear son, now 28 , moved to California's Silicon Valley almost right out of high school and landed one of those sweet jobs in the computer industry. His timing was impeccable. In his eight years there so far, he's already had several pay raises and now makes a bundle of money—far more than his parents have ever made! On this impressive income, he's having a hard time staying on top of his expenses. Our son recently told us that he figured out that the big-bucks jobs aren't what they're cracked up to be. After all the taxes he has to pay on such an income, he's left with a little more than half of what he earns, and that gets handily consumed by the outrageous rent and all of the other incredible expenses of living there. He said that at the cost of living here in Hawai'i, he could live better here on half of what he's earning there.

Here's the good news: He is moving back to Hawai'i this summer! Are we excited? You bet we are!

Our son's story isn't an isolated example, either. Lots of people are in similar positions, if they'd only do the math. In their case, though, they're young and for now at least, many of them like the pace of life there so it's worth it to them. We feel blessed that they are able to see—and talk about—the whole dismal picture of being stuck in what is so aptly called the rat race. Our son is enjoying it for what he can get out of it now, but has no intention to make it his way of life. We have been quietly hoping he would come back home one day.

In Conclusion

One of the unique things about living in Hawai'i is that first of all, if this is your Paradise (as it certainly is for many), you can earn any amount of money (if that is your need) you desire here. If you are even a little bit creative, your income can be directly proportional to your effort. But then, if you have no aspirations to earn lots of money but just want to live a quiet, carefree and beautiful life in the tropics, you can do what we did: figure out what kind of a lifestyle you can afford on however much you know you can easily bring in. We developed our simple lifestyle around our more-or-less fixed retirement income and it's working ever so well. The only time we need hustle up additional funds is for extras, like travel or major purchases. And then we have several income-producing avocations in which we enjoy dabbling when the need arises. We live in a modest-but-beautiful home in the hills of Hilo, within sight of the beautiful Hilo Bay and the always awesome ocean. At this moment, I'm sitting on our lanai with my laptop, enjoying warm, sensuous tropical breezes as I "work." Two laptops, actually. The other one is our kitty, Lucy, who loves to help me type.

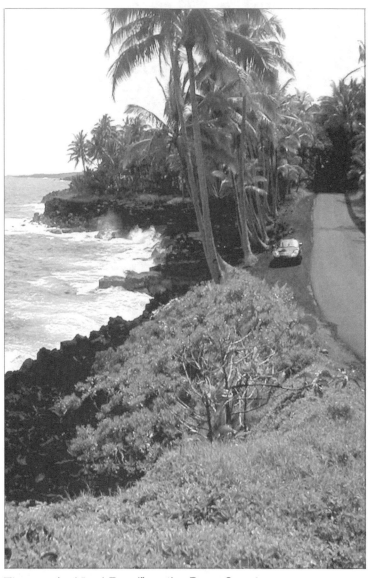

The magical "red Road" on the Puna Coast

Chapter Eight

Retirement Opportunities

Retirement in Hawai'i! What a concept! Many people who have held a straight job for a lot of years also have a monthly retirement check to add to their income, and those over 62 can collect their Social Security payments, as well. None of these by themselves might be significant, but we like living on the "trickle of nickels" system. Nice thing about it is that if one trickle dries up for a while, there are always the others. It just feels a lot more secure to us than to depend on one source of income for all our needs.

Remember, we're talking about the low end of possibilities here, and the kind of lifestyle possible on this minimal kind of an income suits a lot of people very well. Living on less works well in Hawai'i anyway, because when you're here, all of your priorities will shift. New cars and flashy houses just don't seem to matter any longer, nor do stylish fashions or any of hundreds of other drains that normal city-folks have on their incomes. Here, life is about people; friends and family, and the strangers who are just friends you haven't met yet. You'll find yourself spending more time floating in a warm, clear tide pool and less time at cocktail parties; more time at your neighbor's house "talking story" and less time rushing from place to busy place; more time at a comfortable and interesting farmer's market and less time in crowded, noisy (and expensive) malls and supermarkets; and most important, more time at peace with yourself and your environment and less time in the day-to-day struggles so pervasive in city life.

If you have the inclination to start up a small business in Hawai'i, the possibilities are exciting and seem endless. We are constantly amazed by the new and innovative ideas people keep coming up with.

In the last two editions of **Affordable Paradise**, we encouraged establishing a vacation rental—or two. We also encouraged looking intro managing existing vacation rentals that belong to others. Well, things have changed dramatically in the last three or four years here, and now that everyone seems to have the idea of buying a house in Hawai'i and turning it into a vacation rental (gee, what a concept!), there are way more such rentals already than we need. Yes, a lot of them are staying booked, but the impact this process is having on communities is not good.

Until a few months ago, we lived in a beautiful little ocean-front community that over the last few years has changed from a place where about half the homes were occupied by their owners year 'round, and the rest were winter homes for people who lived in cold country and liked to winter here. Some of those homes were occasionally rented as vacation rentals, but most were sporadic and only booked occasionally. Now, the majority of the homes are full-time vacation rentals, managed by very capable folks who keep them booked nearly every day of the year.

So where folks used to know their neighbors, now they get neighbors for a few days and then the next set moves in, and so on. Most of the guests are great people who bother nobody, but some are real party animals and they bother everybody. Thankfully, they are the minority, but still, the ambiance of this little community has changed a lot.

We're no longer encouraging the purchase of homes as vacation rentals, but that certainly isn't going to slow down the trend to do so. What we do encourage, though, is to find ways to earn a living in one of the many spin-offs from this now-huge business.

We have two friends who are partners in a vacation rental management business. They started with nothing but an idea two years ago and now manage about two dozen rentals. They say they could have a hundred if they wanted to, but they have reached the limit of what they feel they can take on without compromising the service they give their clients.

Daily, they get calls from people wanting rental management, and from Realtors who have clients who would buy a home to rent if they were assured somebody to manage it. There is a lot of opportunity here for service-oriented people . . . but be sure that you feel ready, willing and able to serve your clients with much aloha, for that is what is necessary in this business. You'll not only do the advertising and book the guests, but you will be responsible for full management. That includes keeping at the ready your housekeepers, handyman-types to deal with day to day fix-it chores, yard maintenance people, etc. of course, all these sub-jobs get billed to the owners or charged to the guests, whichever is appropriate, but you will be the one who orchestrates the whole show. And it all has to be done in a timely manner, with utmost courtesy and grace.

The compensation is good, because managers charge 25-35% of gross rents, so if one home brings in $2000/month and you are managing 20 of them, you're looking at $10,000/month gross income. One could manage on that, even in Hawai'i!

Your expenses would include consumables, like laundry detergent, toilet paper, paper towels, etc.; advertising; and such niceties as a beautifully arranged vase of fresh tropical flowers for each guest. Your housekeepers get paid out of the cleaning fees charged to your guests. The most successful managers are those who do not skimp or cut corners. They are the ones who make sure their housekeepers do an exemplary job of preparing each rental, that when guests arrive there is soft Hawai'ian music playing, the ceiling fans are going, the lights are on if the guests will be arriving late, and so on. They are the ones who put out more than one roll of paper towels, who present really nice flowers and who call to welcome their guests shortly after their arrival.

It's called aloha; giving back.

You most likely won't need the kind of income you have become used to, you might even consider expanding your favorite pastime or hobby into a business opportunity!

OK, that calls for a little explanation. If we're sounding a bit presumptuous telling you what kind of an income you won't need here, let us again emphasize that this book is written specifically for the folks who are in love with Hawai'i and are looking for an affordable life here. Affordable, by our standards, means a $300,000 house would be a serious stretch. Affordable, by our standards, means a total cost of living of under $2000 a month. And for some, a lot less than that.

There are other books on relocating to Hawai'i that are written for folks of means; the people to whom a $300,000 house is a "starter home." It's unlikely you're in that category since you're still reading this book!

In conclusion, the many friends we've made here who have done just what we've shared in this chapter are living proof that it is not only possible, but even easy. All that is needed is the desire and a little creative planning. After all, we did it, and we like to think of ourselves as beach bums.

Of course, we also have friends still on the Mainland who keep telling us how they are "trapped" there and how much they would love to be able to do what we're doing. We patiently tell them exactly how they could pull it off, but they have all these reasons why it just wouldn't work for them. We believe what's really missing for them is the passion.

As in all endeavors we can think of, the one big key to success is passion.

The bottom line: Our calendar has a "quote for the day" for each day of the year. This morning's quote: "What I truly value, I do." That says it all.

A typical Volcano Village scene

Chapter Nine

Health Care in Hawai'i

The Hawai'i Medical Service Association (HMSA) is the largest provider of health care coverage in the state, and is a nonprofit, mutual benefit society founded in 1938. They provide health plans and employee benefit services. HMSA is led by an executive staff and governed by a 27-member, consumer-oriented board of directors. The board represents a broad cross-section of the local community, including government, business, labor, management, education, finance, the medical profession, religion and the general public. HMSA is a member of the Blue Cross and Blue Shield Association, an association of independent Blue Cross and Blue Shield plans.

Kaiser Permanente is the largest federally qualified, nonprofit HMO in the country and introduced affordable comprehensive coverage to Hawai'i residents in 1958 and now serves more than 215,000 members at the Moanalua Medical Center (on Oahu) and 22 clinics on four islands, including two on the Big Island.

Kaiser Permanente Hawai'i was among only 40 plans out of over 650 HMOs in the United States to receive the prestigious "excellent" accreditation status from the National Committee for Quality Assurance (NCQA).

NCQA is an independent, not-for-profit organization dedicated to assessing and reporting on the quality of managed care plans. (NCQA "excellent" accreditation applies to Kaiser Permanente HMO plans.)

Kaiser Permanente Hawai'i is also accredited by: The Joint Commission on Accreditation of Healthcare Organizations (JCAHO) for their hospital, skilled nursing facility, and home care program; the American College of Radiology for their mammography facilities; and the College of American Pathologists for our laboratories. Other awards received by Kaiser Permanente include:

- ❖ 'Oihana Maika'i, 1996, Kaiser Permanente received the Hawai'i State Award of Excellence to recognize our outstanding commitment to excellence in areas including customer service and satisfaction.
- ❖ Pulama 'Ohana Award, 1996, Kaiser Permanente received this award to recognize how we care for, cherish, and nurture the family.
- ❖ Island Business' "Investing in the Environment" Award, 1996.

Our personal experience with Kaiser Permanente Hawai'i has been excellent in all areas. We like the fact that most services and procedures are covered 100% instead of the usual coverages limited to some percentage of whatever an "approved" amount happens to be, leaving you to pay a large portion of every bill. With Kaiser, there's never a need to figure out the coverages that seem to vary with each service from most providers. When a patient needs medical attention that is beyond the scope of the Big Island's two clinics, Kaiser Permanente flies the patient at Kaiser's expense to the Moanalua Center on Oahu.

There is one thing that recently came to our attention, though, and this is something you might wish to investigate if it applies to you. When you turn 65 and become eligible for Medicare, your benefits from Kaiser change dramatically. At that time, you will lose your dental and vision benefits entirely, and instead of a modest $10 copay on any prescription, you will now get a relatively meaningless 15% discount on the retail price of the prescription. Seems ironic, doesn't it, that Kaiser should shut us down when we might need them the most? Or perhaps that's why they do it. What it all comes down to is when you turn 65, your total dollars going out each month will be about the same as they were when you had your full Kaiser coverage, but you will be receiving substantially less for your money. These "dollars going out" include your Kaiser premium plus your Medicare premium, which is now deducted from your Social Security benefit payment.

Please visit the Web sites listed in the Resource Guide for a complete look at the above medical resources, plus some valuable info on Hawai'i's medical services in general.

Chapter Ten

Final Thoughts

We've covered a lot of ground in these chapters and have had fun doing it. If we've left you more sure about your feelings on moving to Hawai'i, we're thrilled. Actually, whether you're more sure than ever that Hawai'i will be your new home, or if we've helped you discover that you now would like to check out Mexico, it doesn't matter. What is important is that we've helped you become clear on your intentions.

It has been our experience that once we get very clear on what it is we're after, it all seems to fall into place. Every time. On the flip side, if we're confused, can't make up our minds one way or the other, or are even the slightest bit unsure, it's a fight all the way and the odds are stacked against success.

We recommend that in these kinds of decisions, you listen to your heart—your intuition. Sure, there are lots of practical, nuts-and-bolts choices that need to be made when considering a major lifestyle change like this, but the final word should come from a place other than logic. The final decision is not a logical one because moving to Hawai'i is indeed a major lifestyle change. It's not at all comparable to moving from one Mainland state to another, even though that could be a big deal, as well.

At this point, you should have a good feeling of why we say Hawai'i is a lot like a foreign country. As soon as you get settled in and start to allow your life to expand past your personal world and that of your immediate new friends, neighbors and maybe your new work environment, you'll soon find out that everything works differently here.

It is widely understood here that Hawai'i embraces some people and rejects others. With that in mind, we hope that we have given you the tools with which to assess your own Island-Life Compatibility. What we have shared with you in this book is basic inside information from those who have gone before you. It's a glimpse into the future, with somebody else having taken a lot of the bumps for you.

Whether or not you ultimatcly decide to make Hawai'i your own Paradise, it is our sincere hope that we've been of help with your decisions. Wherever life leads you, we wish you brilliant rainbows, spectacular sunsets and much aloha!

Aloha Nui Loa!

*Skip Thomsen
and the Thomsen Ohana*

AFFORDABLE PARADISE

Resource Guide

Newspapers

West Hawai'i Today is Kailua-Kona's Newspaper.
> Web site: www.WestHawai'iToday.com
> Mail contact: Attention: Circulation Department
> P.O. Box 789 Kailua-Kona, Hawai'i 96745-0789
> For more information: Circulation Department, 808-329-9311

Hawai'i Tribune-Herald is Hilo's Newspaper.
> Web site: www.HiloHawaiiTribune.com/
> Subscription   Information: E-mail:
> subscriptions@Hawai'itribuneherald.com

Note: Both of the above newspapers have their classified sections on their Web sites.

Hawai'i Island Journal is Hawai'i Island's independent newspaper.
> P.O. Box 7179, Ocean View, Hawai'i 96737
> Subscription information: 808-328-1951. E-mail: subscribe@Hawaiijournal.com
> **Hawai'i Island Journal** has our recommendation for its straightforward, unbiased reporting of many Island issues, including political, environmental and more.   Included   in   each   issue   is   a

comprehensive calendar of all kinds of events, Island-wide. It's a free paper, published twice a month, and found just about anywhere on the Island. Subscriptions are mailed anywhere.

Real Estate Resources

Hawai'i Information Service

Here's the best, all-inclusive Web site for all of your real-estate needs. The best on-line source for current home and land listings. Check it out and you will be amazed!
www.Hawaiiinformation.com

Hilo Brokers: An excellent Real estate info resource for East Hawai'i: Not updated as often as Hawa'i Information Service, but this site lets you get more specific about the locations you are looking for. Check out their informative Web site: www.hilobrokers.com

West Hawai'i (Kona side) Realtors Web Site: This excellent Web site features a number of different Realtors, all on the Kona side.
www.konaweb.com/real

Two Web sites exclusively for FSBO's

(For Sale By Owner):
www.fsbo-world.com/
www.homeportfoliojunction.com/home/
Hawai'i.htm

Other Real estate Web sites: Type "Big Island real estate," "Hilo real estate," "Big Island for sale by owner," or whatever your imagination inspires into your favorite search utility. Get specific on location if you are interested in only that part of the Island. There are many excellent Web sites covering all areas of the Island.

Tax Records Web Site: This site will give you all of the records available at the property tax office in Hilo, and right on your own computer screen! www.Hawaiipropertytax.com

County Tax Office
(For info on possible real estate purchases)
These folks have a computer available to the public on which you can locate any parcel of land on the Island. All you need is the TMK number. Great resource if you're here looking at property but didn't feel like schlepping your laptop.
865 Pi'ilani Street, Hilo, Hawai'i 96720.
1-808-961-8282
See also: www.Hawaiipropertytax.com

Lenders

Mortgage Brokers come and go here to the point where we no longer recommend any specific ones. You can find all the current ones online by typing in "Hawai'i Mortgage Brokers" and then clicking your way to the Big Island. Also try "Big Island Mortgage Brokers."

More Real estate Resources

Homes & Land. A full-color magazine showing
real estate listings all over the Island. It's available
free in racks outside of restaurants, grocery stores
and elsewhere. You can also see their listings at
www.homes.com. If you'd like your own free
copy, call 1-800-277-7800.

A caveat with this publication is that by the time
listing appear, if they are worthwhile they are long
gone by the time the magazine hits the street. The
main thing we use it for is comparables: staying in
touch with the market.

Title Guaranty Escrow Services
We recommend these folks' very professional and
competent services for your real estate needs: 450
Kilauea Ave., Hilo, Hawai'i 96720. 1-808-935-
6638.

Home Inspections

We do not recommend any particular home
inspectors. The mortgage company you will be
dealing with will probably have a recommendation
for you. There are also quite a few listed in the Big
Island phone directory and on line, too.

Hawai'i Island Street Guides

East Hawai'i Street Guide
Record Copy Service
P.O. Box 11173
Hilo, Hawai'i 96721
(808) 935-0092
E-mail: cbm@ilHawai'i.net

West Hawai'i Street Guide
Swordfish Island Enterprises
75-5595 Palani Rd.,Box #6-152
Kailua-Kona, Hawai'i 96740 (808) 325-6643

The above Street Guides are excellent, cover every
street with detailed maps, and also list all of the
residential subdivisions by name and location. Well
worth the money if you're planning on doing a lot
of house-hunting! They are available at most
Island book stores, some grocery stores and other
locations, as well. The cost is about $10.

Vacation-Rental Web Sites

If you would rather stay in a nicely-furnished home than in
a hotel room (for the same price), check out these Web
sites:
www.A1KapohoVacation.com
www.vrbo.com (Vacation Rentals by Owners)
www.vacationhomes.com
www.hpvacationrentals.com

Each of these Web sites has listings of vacation rentals ranging from humble to luxurious. Simply click your way to the Big Island, and then to the specific location you desire. Another good way to find more sites is to simply type into a search engine the location (Hilo, Puna, etc.) you would like to stay, along with the words vacation rental.

Other Resources

Hawai'i Charter Schools website
http://www.k12.hi.us/~bwoerner/hacs/index.ht
ml

Moving Guide: **So You Want to Live in Hawai'i**
by Toni Polancy. Ms Polancy's book has lots of good nuts-and-bolts info on relocating to Hawai'i. In our opinions, she addresses well-to-do people who would prefer the upscale regions of Maui to rural Hawai'i, but the moving logistics are the same regardless of your Island destination. The book is a good resource. Available from Amazon.com or your local book store.

Shipping

Matson Navigation 1-800-4-MATSON
For your Mainland-to-Hawai'i shipping needs. Visit their excellent Web site for any info you

might need about shipping your belongings and vehicles. www.matson.com

Mihira Transfer 1-808-935-1597

For your Big Island shipping needs. We've had excellent, prompt, courteous and reasonable service from these folks. We recommend them for shipping your container from the Hilo dock to your new home.

DHX Dependable Hawai'ian Express
1-800-488-4888 (Local: 933-7780)

DHX ships between the Islands and Seattle, Portland, Oakland and LA. They will ship either full or partial containers and you have the choice of furnishing your own transport between the docks and your home or they'll go door-to-door. A great solution for you if you don't need a whole container. We've used them for efficient and dependable less-than-container sized shipments.

Shipping Vehicles

Matson Navigation 1-800-4-MATSON

Horizon 1-877-512-2227 (shipmyvehicle.com)

Doing Business in Hawai'i

Business Basics in Hawai'i: Secrets of Starting Your Own Business in Our State, by Dennis K. Kondo. Available from Amazon.com or your local book store.

Department of Motor Vehicles

Motor Vehicles Office/Information: 1-808-961-8351

Phone Companies
Phone Books

Verizon Hawai'i:
> Website: ww.verizon.com. Questions, or ordering a phone book: 1-808-643-3456. Also for ordering phone books: P.O. Box 2200, Honolulu, HI 96841

AT&T: (Recently merged with Cingular) This is the only Cellular service that at this time works in all (well, almost all) areas of the Island. 1-888-289-8722. Local Hilo Store: 333 Kilauea Ave., Hilo, HI 96720. 808-935-9749

Library

Hilo Public Library (Great resource for real
estate TMK maps.) 300 Waianuenue Avenue, Hilo,
Hawai'i 96720. 1-808-933-8888 The library's
entire State-wide catalog is available (the same
screen as you get on the library's own computers)
with a modem connection to 1-808-982-4436. A
real plus!

Rust Protection!

"ACF-50" Here's a product everyone living in Hawai'i
should know about: "ACF-50," also sold as
"Corrosion Guard." Use it on all of your rust-
prone belongings as soon as you get them here! It
absolutely stops corrosion if properly applied to
new metal, and stops the spread of corrosion when
applied to old metal. It's available from Alumside
Products, Inc., 20 Kukila Street, Hilo, Hawai'i
96720. 1-808-935-5485. You can find other
retailers by calling: 1-800-256-2548.

Pet Info

Animal Quarantine Information
The State of Hawai'i's Animal Quarantine Laws:
www.mauibuyersbroker.com/transportation/anim
al.html
State of Hawai'i Department of Agriculture

Animal Quarantine Station
99-951 Halawa Valley Street
Aiea, Hawai'i 96701Telephone (808) 488-8461
www.maui.net/~paradise/events/MHS/
Mauihumane.html

General Hawai'i Information Resource

www.hilo-web.com/phpbb2/
A terrific resource for all sorts of info
about the Hilo side of the Big Island.

www.punaweb.org
Another great resource for all sorts of info
about the Hilo side of the Big Island
specifically focusing on the Puna District.

www.konaweb.com
A wealth of info, specifically about the
Kona side, but also includes a great
resource on moving to the Big Island.

All three of the above sites have Forum Boards in which you can get into discussions with people who live in the subject areas, or just eavesdrop for some valuable insights on what's going on here.

Medical Resources

Hawai'i Health Information Corporation
http://www.hhic.org/index.html

Hawai'i Health Information Corporation
http://www.hhic.org/healthtrends/
healthtrends.html

HMSA, the largest health care provider in Hawai'i
http://www.hmsa.com/

Kaiser Permanente Hawai'i
http://www.kaiserpermanente.org/
locations/hi/

AFFORDABLE PARADISE

About the Author

Skip Thomsen was born and raised in the San Francisco Bay Area and has had an avid interest in writing since childhood. He has written and successfully self-published several books over the last twelve years.

He has also written numerous magazine articles on various how-to topics, including some on relocating to Hawai'i. Reviews of his writing consistently commend him for his ability to make complex topics clear and easy to understand.

During 1988-89, he and his then-wife published an arts-and-entertainment guide called *Elixir!* for the North Oregon Coast area. A paper of 16-20 pages with a circulation of five-thousand copies, it included a variety of articles, fiction, and poetry concerning Oregon Coast issues. It was well received, got great reviews and supported itself from the start with enthusiastic local advertisement. It was put to sleep when Skip moved to Hawai'i in 1993.

Thomsen spent the better part of three years in Hawai'i in the early seventies and knew for certain that this is where he wanted to spend the rest of his life.

Circumstances prompted his move back to the Mainland, but the dream of some day moving to Hawai'i never left him. In 1993, he visited the Islands on his way home from a trip to New Zealand, and for the first time discovered how inexpensive housing was on the Big Island. During that visit, he bought a home there and within a few months had moved to Hawai'i for good.

For these last nine years, friends, visitors, tourists and acquaintances have been making comments like, "How can you afford to live in Hawai'i full time? Isn't it awfully expensive?" To their amazement, Skip and his wife, Camille, would tell them that they live in the Islands for less than the cost of their modest former lifestyles on the Mainland. Of course, everyone wanted to know all the details. Some even recommended Skip write a book on the subject!

There continues to be such a conspicuous amount of interest in affordable living in Hawai'i that the natural next step was *Affordable Paradise*. The first printing sold out quickly and the new material included in the second printings was mostly in response to feedback from the enthusiastic readers of the original book. In addition, Thomsen felt the new Third Edition needed to cover some essential philosophical information that is in response to the changes happening to the Aloha State now that people are moving here in huge numbers.

¶ndex

A

Additional copies of

AFFORDABLE PARADISE

May be ordered from any of the following:

Easy Online Ordering from
the Affordable Paradise Website:
www.AffordableHawaiiLiving.com

For toll-free credit-card phone orders:
1-800-431-1579

Affordable Paradise is also available at
your local bookstore , from **Amazon.com**,
or from any number of on-line booksellers.

**Be sure to visit the Affordable Paradise
Website From time to time to check
for the latest Updates!**

www.AffordableHawaiiLiving.com